APPRENTICE

a year
at the feet
of Jesus

KEITH JOSEPH

www.dustjacket.com

TABLE of CONTENTS

INTRODUCTION

As I begin to write there is an entire empty journal underneath my hand. I have a new journaling Bible as well. I smell its newness and am excited about opening it to begin this year with Jesus. I hear only the sound of my beating heart as I am away from everyone in my office.

I wonder as I sit here: Should I gather other resources for this journey? Would it be valuable to read what others have written about Jesus? I think of taking off the shelf the works of Charles Spurgeon on the life and work of Jesus. I look on the shelf to spot Tim Keller's wonderful read on Jesus' ministry in the gospel of Mark entitled *The King*.

Transparently I have spent too much time over the last few years reading what others have said about Jesus. I need a year in God's Word, at God's table, feasting on life as an apprentice.

This devotion book you hold in your hands is the result of this year's work. I have spent one year day after day laboring over the pages of all four gospels. I have followed Jesus as the King who is coming in Matthew. I have engaged with Jesus in His servant ministry in Mark. I have felt the humanity of Jesus in the gospel of Luke. I have climbed the theological mountain of Jesus as the Son of God in John. I have traced the prophecies in the Old Testament concerning Jesus back to their beginning proclamation points, and I have feasted on the New Testament epistles' understanding of Jesus' life. Finally I have looked to the future of Jesus' second-coming in the book of Revelation.

As you pick up this devotion book you will discover how much I still do not know about Jesus. I pray this devotion does the following for your walk with Jesus as His apprentice:

- I hope this rekindles a passionate love for Jesus (Revelation 2:1-5).
- I hope this opens a door for a simplistic Christ-centered view of ministry (Matthew 16:18).
- I pray the church in America will be revived at the feet of Jesus (2 Timothy 1:7).

Thank you for deciding to walk this journey with Jesus. The outline of the book is simple. You will be given fifty-two devotions. Each comes from the gospel of Mark. Take time to read through the scripture first and the devotion second. Finally, go back through the scripture one more time. Once you have completed this assignment, you will see a five-day scripture reading plan. Each scripture is what Chuck Swindoll calls "the correlation from other passages." You are given questions to answer at the end of each day's reading. By the end of the week you will have gained a greater understanding of what it means to walk as an apprentice of Jesus.

I again thank you for taking this year-long journey with me. I pray the words of Peter over your life this day: "Grow in the grace and knowledge of our Lord and Savior Jesus Christ. To Him be the glory, both now and to the day of eternity. Amen" (2 Peter 3:18, NASB).

WEEK ONE

Choosing the Right Path

Scripture focus: Mark 1:1-11

The beginning of the gospel of Jesus Christ, the Son of God. As it is written in Isaiah the prophet, "Behold, I send my messenger before your face, who will prepare your way, the voice of one crying in the wilderness: 'Prepare the way of the Lord, make his paths straight,'" John appeared, baptizing in the wilderness and proclaiming a baptism of repentance for the forgiveness of sins. And all the country of Judea and all Jerusalem were going out to him and were being baptized by him in the river Jordan, confessing their sins. Now John was clothed with camel's hair and wore a leather belt around his waist and ate locusts and wild honey. And he preached, saying, "After me comes he who is mightier than I, the strap of whose sandals I am not worthy to stoop down and untie. I have baptized you with water, but he will baptize you with the Holy Spirit." In those days Jesus came from Nazareth of Galilee and was baptized by John in the Jordan. And when he came up out of the water, immediately he saw the heavens being torn open and the Spirit descending on him like a dove. And a voice came from heaven, "You are my beloved Son; with you I am well pleased."

As I think about this mission of following Jesus, I cannot help but remember back to those early days of my life when the days of high school were coming to an end. Everyone was focused on a career path. I was no different. I stressed over what I was supposed to do with my life, even though deep inside I knew I was to become an apprentice of Jesus.

I found myself considering all kinds of careers. I settled on teaching simply because a friend of mine was locked into the dream of becoming a teacher. I thought I could do the same. Little did I know that I was about to get on a course that would have destroyed my life had I not changed courses. Now all these years later I think of James warning every generation, "You are a mist that appears for a little while and then vanishes" (James 4:14).

The earlier a person chooses the right path, the longer he or she should enjoy that path.

As we begin our journey together, I want to ask you a very important question: "Have you already chosen the path of following Jesus as His apprentice or are you still deciding?"

Mark, the person God directed to write the gospel of Mark, knew something about the difficulty of following the correct path. We know little of his life from Scripture. But here is what we do know. His mother was holding the prayer meeting on the night Peter was delivered from prison in Acts 12. We know he was an apprentice of Jesus, because why else would his cousin Barnabas want him to follow along with him and Paul as they began their first missionary trip in Acts 13? We also know that for some reason Mark decided to give up on the trip in Acts 13. The turning back of Mark so adversely affected Paul that he refused to allow Mark to go on the next trip, mentioned in Acts 15. Per church history, Peter took Mark under his wing. Mark became a strong leader in the church, to which even Paul gave credit at the end of Paul's life in 2 Timothy 4.

I am amazed as I realize that it is Mark's gospel that has blessed me the most on this year-long journey of becoming an apprentice of Jesus. Mark's life reminds us of this fact: no one is perfect in the journey.

Mark begins his writing with a strong assertion, "Jesus Christ is the Son of God," covering for us the three-plus years of Jesus' ministry. Mark wants us to know this one we are following.

Before anyone can make the correct decision of following someone, he or she needs to know who this person is. So in our first week's readings we are going to cover the first eleven verses of Mark as we seek to make the correct decision to follow Jesus.

Notice what Mark does: He makes us aware of who Jesus is in verse 1. Take time before you go any further in this study and write down on a piece of paper what you know about Jesus.

Mark now begins to walk us down a path of discovery so that we can choose the right path to follow. Pay close attention to the days leading up to Jesus' ministry. Notice the detailed description of John the Baptist's work. Watch with care as Jesus gets baptized. Follow Him into the wilderness of battle and stand tall as you enjoy the kickoff of His ministry.

If you come to this study with questions, here is a good place to begin to have them answered. If you are looking to make sure of a few things, here is a good place to get your answers. This is going to be a journey in which you will not regret your path.

Your devotion and assignment for the week are as follows:

DAY 1:
Read Matthew 1 and answer the following questions.
- Write down Jesus' birthdate. Explain.
- Who was Jesus' father? Explain.

DAY 2:

Read Matthew 2 and answer the following question.

- Why do we not have any references to Jesus' life as a child? Consider in your answer where He grew up.

DAY 3:

Read Luke 1 and answer the following questions.

- Both Mary and Elizabeth had unique pregnancies. What was unique about both?
- What was one main difference?

DAY 4:

Read Luke 2 and answer the following questions.

- Why was Jesus' coming the first and only true hope of peace in the world?
- How did Jesus bring hope into the world?

DAY 5:

Read John 1:1-18 and answer the following questions.

- What does John the Apostle write about Jesus in these verses?
- Did John the Baptist have an important role in Jesus' ministry? Explain.
- What happened to John the Baptist?

How Do You Really Know?

Scripture focus: Mark 1:16-45

*P*assing alongside the Sea of Galilee, he saw Simon and Andrew the brother of Simon casting a net into the sea, for they were fishermen. And Jesus said to them, "Follow me, and I will make you become fishers of men." And immediately they left their nets and followed him. And going on a little farther, he saw James the son of Zebedee and John his brother, who were in their boat mending the nets. And immediately he called them, and they left their father Zebedee in the boat with the hired servants and followed him. And they went into Capernaum, and immediately on the Sabbath he entered the synagogue and was teaching. And they were astonished at his teaching, for he taught them as one who had authority, and not as the scribes. And immediately there was in their synagogue a man with an unclean spirit. And he cried out, "What have you to do with us, Jesus of Nazareth? Have you come to destroy us? I know who you are—the Holy One of God." But Jesus rebuked him, saying, "Be silent, and come out of him!" And the unclean spirit, convulsing him and crying out with a loud voice, came out of him. And they were all amazed, so that they questioned among themselves, saying, "What* *is this? A new teaching with authority! He commands even the unclean spirits, and they obey him." And at once his fame spread everywhere throughout all the surrounding region of Galilee. And immediately he left the synagogue and entered the house of Simon and Andrew, with James and John. Now Simon's mother-in-law lay ill with a fever, and immediately they told him about her. And he came and took her by the hand and lifted her up, and the fever left her, and she began to serve them. That evening at sundown they brought to him all who were sick or oppressed by demons. And the whole city was gathered together at the door. And he healed many who were sick with various diseases, and cast out many demons. And he would not permit the demons to speak, because they knew him. And rising very early in the morning, while it was still dark, he departed and went out to a desolate place, and there he prayed. And Simon and those who were with him searched for him, and they found him and said to him, "Everyone is looking for you." And he said to them, "Let us go on to the next towns, that I may preach there also, for that is why I came out." And he went throughout all Galilee, preaching in their synagogues and casting out demons. And a leper came to him, imploring him, and kneeling said to him, "If you will, you can make me clean." Moved with pity, he stretched out his hand and touched him and said to him, "I will; be clean." And immediately the leprosy left him, and he was made clean. And Jesus[d] sternly charged him and sent him away at once, and said to him, "See that you say nothing to anyone, but go, show yourself to the priest and offer for your cleansing what Moses commanded, for a proof to them." But he went out and began to talk freely about it, and to spread the news, so that Jesus could no longer openly enter a town, but was out in desolate places, and people were coming to him from every quarter.*

The decision to follow Jesus has been made. You are in the group commonly known as "Christian." Perhaps your first day as a Christian was filled with all kinds of handshakes, congratulations, and the wonderful "If you need anything let me know." But now it is crunch time. You are going to actually be an apprentice of Jesus.

I think this is a very good spot for a question: "Do you really know what you're getting into with Jesus?"

When it comes to what we know about most things, one of three frames of reference form our viewpoints:

- **The indoctrination from birth**. You were constantly told in so many words, "This is the best way to live, and this is the best person to follow." Admission: the reason my kids are University of Kentucky basketball fans is because their dad indoctrinated them. Sometimes this is a good thing, in my case especially. At other times this is a bad thing when a person follows the wrong path.

- **The incorporation of many views**. Most people form their worldview based upon the work and influence of many people. It could have been what the professor said, the pastor said, or one's best friend said. In first grade I was always in trouble because my chosen friend was ADHD.

- **The investigation and settled view**. Some people take the time to detox from both indoctrination and incorporation. Such people study for themselves and arrive at a settled position. Romans 4:5 says, "Each one should be fully convinced in his own mind."

If you and I are going to get the most out of our apprenticeship, we have to become hands-on with the Scripture. So let's begin by opening our Bibles to the Scripture focus for this week. Now let's get to work in finding out what it means to be an apprentice of Jesus.

As we read this week and as we follow Jesus, two principles will govern our time with Jesus:

1. To start correctly in a new position, you have to exit the previous position fully.

Think about Jesus' ministry to this point. Everything He did was new to the people who encountered Him. Later in our studies Jesus will so impress the High Priests' detectives that they will report, "We never heard a man teach this way before".

Pay close attention as Jesus calls out to four men. Look at the waves as they crash into the shoreline. Notice the rugged look of four men whose sin has hardened them from extended exposure to the sun. Notice their weather-beaten faces and calloused hands. These were common men.

Jesus calls out, "Follow me, and I will make you become fishers of men" (Mark 1:17). Jesus is compelling them to come to a new position. This position is a direct line from where they were previously. Imagine what they had to give up. They had to leave jobs, careers, families, what was familiar, and even their homes. But they immediately followed.

2. To stick it out in the new position, you have to embrace the new position fully.

These four men made a direct course to Jesus with a mindset of "I'm all in." This must be our mind-set, because the enemy will do his best to convince you of the foolish decision you have just made. New opportunities will appear before you. You'll tempted to think, "I really didn't think this through." Your mind will begin to reason with you: "If I had known of these opportunities, I might not have chosen this direction this year."

Stick it out. You're about to spend a year with Jesus, who will be teaching with power unlike you've ever seen. The moments will be real, relevant, and exciting. You will tangle with demons, minister to thousands, watch as Jesus shows compassion at a level you've never before witnessed. This is just the beginning. What you will see will make what you are being offered seem small in comparison.

So decide now to embrace this new position. Let's go! Here are our assignments for the week:

DAY 1:

Read John 1:19-50 and answer the following questions.
- Describe your relationship with Jesus. Would you describe yourself as one of the following: saved, a Christ follower, authentic, a friend, or other? Explain.
- What miracles have you experienced so far in your journey with Christ? Write down a few of them.

DAY 2:

Read I Kings 19 and Luke 9:57-62 and answer the following questions.
- What things have you had to give up in order to follow Jesus? Explain.
- What teachings of Jesus have been the hardest to obey? Explain.

DAY 3:

Read John 1:1-5, Psalm 119:1-9, and Hebrews 4 and answer the following questions.
- Why is it important for the apprentice to listen daily to Jesus' teaching?
- What have you learned from today's reading?

DAY 4:

Read Acts 14 and complete the following assignments.

- Spend time seeking God's heart concerning the issues facing our world today. Write down what you have discovered.
- What types of needs do you see before you this day? Write down your answers and commit them to prayer:

DAY 5:

Read Ephesians 5 and answer the following questions.

- Do you find yourself in a rut or endless routine? Explain.
- How would a year with Jesus change all of this? Spend the weekend seeking the answer.

Taking the Roof Off

Scripture focus: Mark 2:1-17

A nd when he returned to Capernaum after some days, it was re-ported that he was at home. And many were gathered together, so that there was no more room, not even at the door. And he was preaching the word to them. And they came, bringing to him a paralytic carried by four men. And when they could not get near him because of the crowd, they removed the roof above him, and when they had made an opening, they let down the bed on which the paralytic lay. And when Jesus saw their faith, he said to the paralytic, "Son, your sins are forgiven." Now some of the scribes were sitting there, questioning in their hearts, "Why does this man speak like that? He is blaspheming! Who can forgive sins but God alone?" And immediately Jesus, perceiving in his spirit that they thus questioned with-in themselves, said to them, "Why do you question these things in your hearts? Which is easier, to say to the paralytic, 'Your sins are forgiven,' or to say, 'Rise, take up your bed and walk'? But that you may know that the Son of Man has authority on earth to forgive sins"—he said to the paralytic— "I say to you, rise, pick up your bed, and go home." And he rose and im-

mediately picked up his bed and went out before them all, so that they were all amazed and glorified God, saying, "We never saw anything like this!"

He went out again beside the sea, and all the crowd was coming to him, and he was teaching them. And as he passed by, he saw Levi the son of Alphaeus sitting at the tax booth, and he said to him, "Follow me." And he rose and followed him.

And as he reclined at table in his house, many tax collectors and sinners were reclining with Jesus and his disciples, for there were many who followed him. And the scribes of the Pharisees, when they saw that he was eating with sinners and tax collectors, said to his disciples, "Why does he eat with tax collectors and sinners?" And when Jesus heard it, he said to them, "Those who are well have no need of a physician, but those who are sick. I came not to call the righteous, but sinners."

Week three has rolled around, and we're feeling the weight of all of this apprentice work. It's every day with Jesus. It's every moment with the mind and spirit engaged in this commitment. The tendency is to think, "Just one day off, Jesus--that's all I ask."

As we come to Mark 2, I believe the original apprentices must have felt the same way. I believe they were ready for a break. They were already struggling to have alone time with Jesus.

Jesus' focus was clearly to advance the apprentices, because the cross was coming and Jesus' work would be over in three short years. The work of the church would come before the apprentices soon enough. It was now time to go back to a familiar place where Jesus was staying with friends. But it was about to change.

Just for a moment I want to take a sidebar second to make you aware of something you may not already know. Jesus often takes His apprentices to two places as He is preparing them. One of those places is defined as desolate. Do not be discouraged by this word. It speaks rest and refreshment to those who get to be alone with Jesus. The sec-

12

ond place is what I call a defining place. It is in such a place that most apprentices find mile markers that define who they will become.

It is to this second place Jesus and His apprentices find themselves in Mark 2. According to Luke 5:17, Jesus is teaching a mixed crowd. There are those who are hurting in the crowd. There are those who are conceited in the crowd. And there are those who are inquisitive in the crowd. But for a moment look away from the crowd.

Five guys approach the house where Jesus is staying. Not the Five Guys who own a restaurant by that name, even though I would be willing to meet there with Jesus. Four of these guys are healthy, and one has been paralyzed by a sickness.

One thing is clear: they have real saving faith. When Jesus makes the proclamation "Thy sins are forgiven," we know God forgives only those who evidence faith in Jesus and repentance of sins (Romans 10:9-13). These men came with an anticipating faith that would take the roof off the meeting they were in.

The guys quickly access the situation and determine that they cannot get to Jesus by conventional ways. So they become creative. Their faith takes them to the rooftop. Their faith leads to sacrifice in tearing off part of the roof. I wonder, when did Jesus stop teaching? Was it when they first started to work or somewhere in the middle? I think somewhere in the middle, at a good stopping point, Jesus stops. All eyes turn to the roof as light breaks through. Now they see four guys. Was this a robbery or terrorism? Suddenly the men put a stretcher over the hole, and now with ropes they lead the man down to the ground in front of Jesus. This is a taking-the-roof-off moment.

Listen to me: if we're going to take the roof off in our faith, there are moments when conventional wisdom will not be enough.

Two governing rooftop facts:

1. Faith will remove the roof of doubt, discouragement, and do not's.

When Jesus said, "Your sins are forgiven," I imagine those four guys shouting for joy. I imagine the peace that must have come to this man's mind and heart.

Their faith took the roof off. They understood that forgiveness of sins was possible because of Jesus (Ephesians 1:7).

The first and greatest miracle is the miracle of salvation given to the lame man. The second miracle, which is a lesser miracle, is sometimes wrongly thought to be the greater.

2. Faith will remove the roof of all disease, darkness, and deceit.

Jesus heals the man. Now the room is silent as this man gets up and walks out before them. I can just see the four guys starting to scramble off the roof. One shouts, "Jesus, we'll put the roof back on in the morning!" Another shouts, "There's no God like our God!" Now we hear all of them singing "Victory in Jesus."

The disease is gone!

Now look back into the room. See the leaders filled with deceit. The darkness in their hearts could not overcome the light of the world, John 8:12. Five guys took the roof off this meeting because of their faith in Jesus.

We understand that "Jesus takes the roof off." We simply have faith by starting to move forward. Faith is unstoppable. If you don't believe me, just read Matthew 9:9-13. Matthew's story is also a taking-the-roof-off story.

Here are our assignments for the week:

DAY 1:
Read Luke 5 and answer the following questions.
- How valuable is alone time with Jesus? Explain.
- What doubts are you keeping from Jesus in your alone time? Write them here:

DAY 2:

Read John 4 and answer the following questions.

- How does it feel to be pronounced "forgiven" by Jesus? Explain.
- What creative ways can God use you to get the gospel to other people? Write your answers.
-

DAY 3:

Read Romans 3 and answer the following questions.

- What obstacles in your life could a miracle of faith change? Write your answers.
- How will you use the story of the miracles you experience to glorify God? Write your answers.

DAY 4:

Read Matthew 9 and answer the following questions.

- How can God use your career as a mission point? Explain.
- Do you need a career change or a heart change? Explain.

DAY 5:

Read Romans 9 and engage with the following exercises.

- Spend extra time in prayer for your friends and coworkers today. Write their names and what God said about each.
- Make a list of faith things you want to see God to take the roof off. Share them with others.

WEEK FOUR

What Happens on Sunday?

Scripture focus: Mark 2:23--3:6

*O*ne *Sabbath he was going through the grainfields, and as they made their way, his disciples began to pluck heads of grain. And the Pharisees were saying to him, "Look, why are they doing what is not lawful on the Sabbath?" And he said to them, "Have you never read what David did, when he was in need and was hungry, he and those who were with him: how he entered the house of God, in the time of Abiathar the high priest, and ate the bread of the Presence, which it is not lawful for any but the priests to eat, and also gave it to those who were with him?" And he said to them, "The Sabbath was made for man, not man for the Sabbath. So the Son of Man is lord even of the Sabbath."*

Again he entered the synagogue, and a man was there with a withered hand. And they watched Jesus, to see whether he would heal him on the Sabbath, so that they might accuse him. And he said to the man with the withered hand, "Come here." And he said to them, "Is it lawful on the Sabbath to do good or to do harm, to save life or to kill?" But they were silent. And he looked around at them with anger, grieved at their hardness of heart, and said to the man, "Stretch out your hand." He stretched it out, and his hand was restored. The Pharisees went out and immediately held counsel with the Herodians against him, how to destroy him.

It was fun for Heather at first. She loved all the relationships she developed in the church. The members were good people. They took care of one another. But things changed for Heather. She attended her church's business meeting and quickly discovered the deadlock in the congregation. The pastor was trying to direct them to reach younger families in the community. One leader rejected the pastor's suggestions with a stingy accusation: "I don't know why you're always talking about people who aren't members of our church. This is our church, and our needs come first." Tom Rainer writes on pages 4-5 in his book I Will, "Heather joined the church expecting to make a difference. But now that seemed impossible."

Question: What happens at your church on Sunday? One precious saint thought back to the tough days of her church's past and commented, "I used to dread going to church."

Every longtime card-carrying church member has horror stories of tough times. But a Christ-centered church will work through them. This week's devotions seek to look deeply into what Jesus taught His apprentices concerning the subject of the Lord's Day.

Mark gives us two examples from Jesus' ministry concerning what was happening on the Sabbath day. I spent some time researching how many times the gospels speak of Jesus' work on the Sabbath. Recorded in the Gospels, there are nine different Sabbath days on which Jesus ministered. Here is what Jesus did on the Sabbath:

He taught; He visited in homes; He cast out demons; He forgave sin; He healed people; He debated on the Sabbath; and He was always condemned by the religious leaders for His work on the Sabbath.

What is your church doing on Sunday?

This scene in Mark 2 shows us how terrible the Sabbath day had become. What God had intended to be an amazing day had become an agonizing day. The religious leaders had added thirty-nine acts that were strictly forbidden on the Sabbath. Moses had simply prohibited work on the Sabbath (Exodus 20:10). The religious leaders in their minds brought clarity to the day!

Pay attention as you read Jesus' responses to their condemnation. God intends for His day to be valuable to each of us in these ways as we enter His house:

a. A place of prayer (Isaiah 56:7)

b. A place with an altar (I Kings 8:29-38; example in 2 Kings 18–19)c. A place of release and rest (Matthew 28:18-20)

d. A place of power (1 Corinthians 16:19-20)

e. A place of instruction (Luke 6:1-2)

f. A place of fellowship (Acts 2:42-46)

The Lord's day is to be an amazing day in our lives. We see God's power illustrated by Mark's account of another Sabbath day in 3:1-6. Take time to walk through the illustration noticing the difference between Jesus' heart and the hearts of the Pharisees.

Decide for yourself: is it lawful to do good or to harm, to save or to kill?

While in Malawi last year I shared this passage with the pastors in our yearly conference. It was easy to see the conviction of God as one pastor evidenced when he said, "We need a change at our church on Sundays!"

Spend time with the Lord as you work through this week's devotions and ask Him, What do You want to do in my life on Your day?

Here are our assignments for the week:

DAY 1:

Read Exodus 20:8-11; Leviticus 23, and answer the following questions.

- What were God's guidelines for the Sabbath?
- What problems would you have in keeping the Sabbath laws? Explain.

DAY 2:

Read Hosea 6; Luke 4, and answer the following questions.

- What causes people to feel either loved or unloved in the church? Explain.
- Describe what mercy would look like in your church's worship services.

DAY 3:

Read Matthew 12; Luke 6, and answer the following questions.

- How does a hard heart affect the worship service? Explain.
- What miracles need to take place in your church?

DAY 4:

Read Colossians 2 and answer the following questions.

- Name some traditions that are harmful to the body of Christ.
- Name a tradition that has helped you to know God more. Explain.

DAY 5:

Read Matthew 5 and answer the following questions.

- How could the Beatitudes give freedom to our worship?
- How does forgiveness affect worship in church?

The Twenty-First-Century Jesus

Scripture focus: Mark 3:7-12

Jesus withdrew with his disciples to the sea, and a great crowd followed, from Galilee and Judea and Jerusalem and Idumea and from beyond the Jordan and from around Tyre and Sidon. When the great crowd heard all that he was doing, they came to him. And he told his disciples to have a boat ready for him because of the crowd, lest they crush him, for he had healed many, so that all who had diseases pressed around him to touch him. And whenever the unclean spirits saw him, they fell down before him and cried out, "You are the Son of God." And he strictly ordered them not to make him known.

This week's Scripture focus places us in a moment that most people who grew up in small towns would not have experienced. As Jesus pulls His apprentices away from the city, we find a great crowd following Him down to the seashore.

We do not know how large the crowd was, but we do know that Mark describes it as "a great crowd." In my lifetime I have been in some great crowds. I have been in crowds where people were pushing to get into a major sporting event. I have seen (from a distance!) crowds where people stood in line for days to get the best seats for a concert. I once remember almost getting crushed in a Romanian Gypsy village as we were simply giving out travel-sized soap, toothpaste, and shampoo. But never was I in a crowd like the one described in Mark 3.

Some people were desperate in the crowd. Others were filled with demonic spirits. Still others were there to get what they wanted. Each came with elevated emotions.

As I thought of this moment, I began considering what people could possibly visualize and theorize about Jesus today. C. S. Lewis wrote the following in his amazing work Mere Christianity:

I am trying here to prevent anyone saying the foolish thing that people often say about Him: "I'm ready to accept Jesus as a great moral teacher, but I don't accept His claim to be God." That is the one thing we must not say. A man who said the sort of things Jesus said would not be a great moral teacher. He would either be a lunatic--on a level with the man who says he is a poached egg--or else he would be the Devil of Hell. You must make your choice. Either this man was, and is, the Son of God: or else a madman or something worse. You can shut Him up for a fool, you can spit at Him and kill Him as a demon; or you can fall at His feet and call Him Lord and God. But let us not come with any patronizing nonsense about His being a great human teacher. He has not left that open to us. He did not intend to.

All of this leads me to a burning question: "Is the twenty-first-century Jesus being proclaimed the same as the Jesus Mark proclaimed?"

The crowds who followed Jesus from all four corners of Palestine came with the goal of Jesus' healing them. Mark wrote simply that they followed him The word followed is not the same word as given to describe the apprentices' following Jesus. It simply refers to the crowds' coming behind him. They followed because of the events they had heard about. They knew of Jesus' episodes of healing.

Jesus did not embrace this type of fanfare. Today we sometimes see crowds coming to large gatherings, and we are prone to question, "Why are they there?"

Some crowds are filled with people who are there for the wrong reasons:

- They blindly believe Jesus exists to be their Bank of America.
- They purposely are deceived by those who exploit them (2 Timothy 3:4-7).
- They openly are led to destruction by those who practice a false gospel (2 Peter 2).

But many other crowds are following the same Jesus whom Mark followed:

- They are being drawn by God (John 6:34-35; 2 Corinthians 4:4-6).
- They are clearly following godly pastors (2 Timothy 4:1-2).
- They are weekly being discipled in the Word of God (2 Timothy 2:15; Ephesians 4:11-16).

This week's assignments will lead you to consider your role in making sure the world knows who Jesus is.

Here are our assignments for the week:

DAY 1:
Read Matthew 5 and answer the following questions.
- Why are the Beatitudes so important to our genuine salvation experience? Explain.
- When Jesus said that our righteousness must "[exceed] that of the scribes and Pharisees" (Matthew 5:20), He was referring to what?

DAY 2:

Read Isaiah 42 and answer the following questions.

- In Matthew 12:15-21 did Jesus fulfill the prophecy of Isaiah 42? Give examples.
- In our focal text we read of the sick freely coming to Jesus. Why was this the case?

DAY 3:

Read Luke 6 and answer the following questions.

- Now that you have read some of Jesus teaching and His compassion, what does it motivate you to do?
- Considering Luke 6:46-49, write down the reasons people need a Savior.

DAY 4:

Read John 5 and answer the following questions.

- Did the man who was healed by the pool profess Jesus as his Lord and Savior? Give reasons for your answer.
- Why were the Jews wanting to kill Jesus in verse 18?

DAY 5:

Read Revelation 1 and answer the following questions.

- Why was John on the Isle of Patmos, and what might this look like in our lives today?
- Try to describe the resurrected Jesus from the description given in Revelation 1.

A Strange Group

Scripture focus: Mark 3:13-21, 31-35

*A*nd he went up on the mountain and called to him those whom he desired, and they came to him. And he appointed twelve (whom he also named apostles) so that they might be with him and he might send them out to preach and have authority to cast out demons. He appointed the twelve: Simon (to whom he gave the name Peter); James the son of Zebedee and John the brother of James (to whom he gave the name Boanerges, that is, Sons of Thunder); Andrew, and Philip, and Bartholomew, and Matthew, and Thomas, and James the son of Alphaeus, and Thaddaeus, and Simon the Zealot, and Judas Iscariot, who betrayed him. Then he went home, and the crowd gathered again, so that they could not even eat. And when his family heard it, they went out to seize him, for they were saying, "He is out of his mind." . . .*

And his mother and his brothers came, and standing outside they sent to him and called him. And a crowd was sitting around him, and they said to him, "Your mother and your brothers are outside, seeking you." And he answered them, "Who are my mother and my brothers?" And looking about at those who sat around him, he said, "Here are my mother and my brothers! For whoever does the will of God, he is my brother and sister and mother."

One of my favorite books in recent years has been the book by John MacArthur entitled Twelve Ordinary Men. The book shares detailed and accurate information about the lives of each of the disciples. The one disciple I so want to know more about is Simon the Zealot.

Very little has been written about his life. From Scripture we know he was a very zealous man, of course. But for the rest we must rely on history. Most believe he was certainly a part of the group of politically minded Zealots. MacArthur writes, "The Zealots hated the Romans, and their goal was to overthrow the Roman occupation. They advanced their agenda primarily through terrorism and surreptitious acts of violence" (174).

Now pay close attention to this fact: One of the members of the group was Matthew, who was a former tax collector. On Simon's list of people he would have hated would have been anyone who sold out the people to gain money from Rome. The truth is, "Simon would have wanted to take Matthew out and could have had him on his list, that is, until he met Jesus."

Brothers and sisters, these men made up a strange group. But so is the case of the church itself, which has always been made up of people from all walks and ways of life.

This week in our studies we are diving into the beauty of the strong group called the body of Christ. As I wrote this devotion I was waiting to have my wisdom tooth extracted. I sat there and thought of all the people who were going to be involved in this surgical procedure. There was my loving wife on the front end encouraging me and on the back end to care for me when it was over. Along the path were receptionists, nurses, technicians, and a great oral surgeon. Each had his or her part.

Each was placed in my path by a loving God who works all things for His good.

Consider for a moment Jesus, who was calling these men together. In Luke's account Jesus prayed all night before He chose the twelve to be his Apostles.

I wrote the following in the margin of my Bible: "Jesus always selects disciples." Each of these disciples had different works awaiting them in God's kingdom work. They came from different walks of life having done things in different ways. Each of these men was chosen because of the gifts, talents, and experiences he possessed. Even Judas was chosen by God for the task of betrayal. I want you to think deeply as you study this week about how God wants to use your unique abilities to grow His kingdom.

I also wrote in the margin of my Bible, "Jesus had specific discipleship methods for His apprentices." Jesus would spend three years personally investing in these men. He would show them how to minister His word and to do His work. He would have sent them out on trial missions to get an understanding of the power at work in those who do His will.

Finally I wrote, "Jesus also suffered through specific discouraging moments." In our reading today we find his own early family not understanding the call on his life. They took one look at the team he had assembled to accomplish the task and thought, "He's out of His mind." Brothers and sisters, this is the way it is with people who do not understand the beauty of the church. Our God takes nobodies and magnifies himself in their lives leading them to a do works that are amazing.

As you read, be ready for the discouraging moments--but also be reading for the defining moments as you are called to a strange group--the group called the church. This group is touching the world with the gospel.

Here are our assignments for the week:

DAY 1:

Read Luke 6 and complete the following items.

- Take time to look up the names of the twelve disciples, and chose two to write a few descriptive sentences about.
- List some common excuses people give for not wanting to serve the Lord.

DAY 2:

Read Job 1–2 and answer the following questions.

- Why did the leaders chosen by Jesus have such difficult backgrounds? Explain.
- How can a person overcome the attacks of Satan? Explain.

DAY 3:

Read Ephesians 4 and answer the following questions.

- What gifts and talents do you possess?
- Are there specific ways the Lord is dealing with you about serving Him? Explain.

DAY 4:

Read Mathew 6–7 and answer the following questions.

- Are you asking God for power in any area of your life? Explain:
- What training would help you grow in your spiritual life? Explain.

DAY 5:

Read John 7 and answer the following questions.

- What type of special connection do you have with the brothers and sisters in your church? Explain.
- Do you ever face persecution from your family and friends because of your faith? Explain.

WEEK SEVEN

Danger

Scripture focus: Mark 3:22-30

And the scribes who came down from Jerusalem were saying, "He is possessed by Beelzebub," and "by the prince of demons he casts out the demons." And he called them to him and said to them in parables, "How can Satan cast out Satan? If a kingdom is divided against itself, that kingdom cannot stand. And if a house is divided against itself, that house will not be able to stand. And if Satan has risen up against himself and is divided, he cannot stand, but is coming to an end. But no one can enter a strong man's house and plunder his goods, unless he first binds the strong man. Then indeed he may plunder his house.

"Truly, I say to you, all sins will be forgiven the children of man, and whatever blasphemies they utter, but whoever blasphemes against the Holy Spirit never has forgiveness, but is guilty of an eternal sin"— for they were saying, "He has an unclean spirit."

We have all been exposed to them! Each of us, depending where we live, have walked right by them. I suspect we have even gotten closer to them than we care to admit. You ask, "What are you talking about?" I am referring to those simple things we call "danger signs" or "warning signs."

I think about the many days I spent in the yard with my two boys passing football or playing a game. Each time there was in the edge of our lot an electrical transformer that had the ability to kill each of us if we failed to pay attention to the sign. For five plus years I mowed the grass right beside this transformer. I never thought of it until right now. If I had opened the transformer covering, I could have been instantly killed. How often do we live our lives without thinking about the grace given to us by others in their efforts to warn us of danger?

In a much greater way Jesus in Mark 3 offers to His constant opponents a warning sign. I believe what others have written that they had not crossed the line but were well on their way. You ask, "What were they on their way to doing?" Answer--blaspheming against the Holy Spirit.

To blaspheme means to deliberately speak in a way to injure or destroy the one you are speaking against.

In the context of our reading it is easy to see that the religious leaders were desiring to destroy Jesus. In this setting their blasphemous speech centered around the accusation of Jesus' being on the devil's team. These leaders accused Jesus of working miracles in the power of Satan.

Jesus offered two responses: One in parables (verses 23-27) and the other in direct teaching (verses 28-30).

First we read the parables. Jesus illustrates the ridiculous view of being against someone while attempting success on the same team. It is impossible for a marriage to be successful unless both husband and wife are working together. It is impossible for a nation to be successful if the people are working against each other. Jesus' point is clear: "I am standing against Satan, so it is clear that I am not on his team."

Jesus continues to enlighten them concerning the point by describing how hard it is to overcome someone's enemy. Unless you have the strength to overcome him, you're fighting a useless battle. The point was clear: the religious leaders were fighting a losing battle.

If they would just turn to Jesus, they would discover His power over the enemy. In your readings this week you will see firsthand the strength of the battle and the power we have in Christ to overcome.

Second, we come to the direct teaching. Jesus cries to these leaders, "Danger--you are about to cross the line of no return." The religious leaders had said and were continuing to say many things against Jesus. As they did this they were continuing to harden their heart to what He was saying in the power of the Holy Spirit.

If they continued to reject Jesus, there would come a time when they would be so hardened that they would never receive Jesus as Lord and Savior. Jesus says, "If you come to this place there will never be the opportunity for you to get into heaven."

If you keep up this line of thinking, you're going to cross a line of no return. I truly believe hell has many residents who at one time sat in a children's Sunday School class or sang in a children's choir. I believe hell has many residents who owned a Bible when they were alive. I believe it has preachers and seminary professors who simply taught what they grew to believe no longer.

In this week's readings you will be challenged to work through what you believe, and you will be challenged to make sure your heart, mind, and ears are attentive to what Jesus says.

Maybe you're thinking about someone else in terms of our study. Take time to pray for him or her this week and take time to study deeply this truth. Then ask God to open a door for you to be able to share with those who are ignoring the danger signs.

Here are our assignments for the week.

DAY 1:

Read John 14:20-26; 16:7-11, 14; and Titus 3:1-5, and answer the following questions.

- What is the job of the Holy Spirit according to Scripture?
- What role does the Holy Spirit play in the salvation of people?

DAY 2:

Read 1 Samuel 15 and answer the following questions.

- Was God unfair with Saul in removing him from leadership? Explain.
- Was Saul a true believer or not? Explain.

DAY 3:

Read Isaiah 7 and answer the following questions.

- What was Satan's problem in serving the Lord? Explain.
- What if any problems do you and I have with serving the Lord?

DAY 4:

Read Acts 8 and answer the following questions.

- What role did the Holy Spirit play in Philip's ministry?
- Did Simon blaspheme against the Holy Spirit? Explain.

DAY 5:

Read Hebrews 6 and Hebrews 10:26-29 and answer the following questions.

- Can a person lose his or her salvation? Explainr.
- Do you ever feel as if you are not a Christ follower? Interact with your study group in giving your answer.

WEEK EIGHT

Listening

Scripture focus: Mark 4:1-25

*A*gain *he began to teach beside the sea. And a very large crowd gathered about him, so that he got into a boat and sat in it on the sea, and the whole crowd was beside the sea on the land. And he was teaching them many things in parables, and in his teaching he said to them: "Listen! Behold, a sower went out to sow. And as he sowed, some seed fell along the path, and the birds came and devoured it. Other seed fell on rocky ground, where it did not have much soil, and immediately it sprang up, since it had no depth of soil. And when the sun rose, it was scorched, and since it had no root, it withered away. Other seed fell among thorns, and the thorns grew up and choked it, and it yielded no grain. And other seeds fell into good soil and produced grain, growing up and increasing and yielding thirtyfold and sixtyfold and a hundredfold." And he said, "He who has ears to hear, let him hear."*

And when he was alone, those around him with the twelve asked him about the parables. And he said to them, "To you has been given the secret of the kingdom of God, but for those outside everything is in parables, so that

*"'they may indeed see but not perceive,
and may indeed hear but not understand,
lest they should turn and be forgiven.'"*

And he said to them, "Do you not understand this parable? How then will you understand all the parables? The sower sows the word. And these are the ones along the path, where the word is sown: when they hear, Satan immediately comes and takes away the word that is sown in them. And these are the ones sown on rocky ground: the ones who, when they hear the word, immediately receive it with joy. And they have no root in themselves, but endure for a while; then, when tribulation or persecution arises on account of the word, immediately they fall away. And others are the ones sown among thorns. They are those who hear the word, but the cares of the world and the deceitfulness of riches and the desires for other things enter in and choke the word, and it proves unfruitful. But those that were sown on the good soil are the ones who hear the word and accept it and bear fruit, thirtyfold and sixtyfold and a hundredfold."

And he said to them, "Is a lamp brought in to be put under a basket, or under a bed, and not on a stand? For nothing is hidden except to be made manifest; nor is anything secret except to come to light. If anyone has ears to hear, let him hear." And he said to them, "Pay attention to what you hear: with the measure you use, it will be measured to you, and still more will be added to you. For to the one who has, more will be given, and from the one who has not, even what he has will be taken away."

As you open your copy of God's Word to Mark 4, I point you to a one-word command given by Jesus. Notice as the word listen appears as the first word of verse three. Say the word out loud. Say it again: listen.

Jesus spoke this one-word command to the crowds who had gathered on the shores of the Sea of Galilee. He had gotten in a small fishing vessel and pushed out a little in the water because the water would carry his voice so clearly to the untold numbers who were gathered. The Bible does not tell us whether the apprentices were in the boat with Him or if they remained on the shore. I think they were probably in the boat with Him.

The audience was diverse. You had those who were always in the crowd. They seemed to hang on every word spoken by the living Word. There were the usual onlookers who wanted to see how many people He would heal on this day. Others had come a long distance with the hope of being touched by the Lord's hands. Still others were getting more and more skeptical about His ministry. Then there were those who were there for the first time. These people had not yet made up their minds. They were thinking, "Who is this one whom others are calling the Messiah?"

I have been so many times faced with diverse crowds. As a pastor I have experienced people who took every note and asked questions. I have wondered about those who come but never seem to engage. I have seen those who occasionally come but about whom I know very little. Still yet, there are so many about whom I wonder, What are they taking in?

Consider this truth: "Those who grow in Christ must develop the art of listening."

Those original apprentices were taught from day one that they must listen. If these men failed to listen, they were going to miss over half of their training. Are you a good listener?

The responses to this question will vary:

- Some people respond, "I don't like to listen" (that is, read God's Word).

- Some people respond, "I'm a hands-on person."

- Some people respond, "What's the purpose

in listening?"

- Some people respond, "I love to listen."

As you consider Jesus' teaching in Mark 4, it's important for you to listen. We see this so much being lived out in the apprentices' lives after Jesus returned to heaven. We read of moments when they're recorded as saying, "We remember what the Lord said to us."

As Jesus spoke to the crowds He used a teaching devise we know as parables. A parable is simply a story laid beside a truth to clarify the meaning in a practical way. Jesus' parable on the three types of soil in Mark 4 is perhaps the most well-known and widely taught parable.

The parable given by Jesus is clear: "The condition of the soil affects the return of the seed planted." The truth of the parable is clear: "The condition of the heart affects the return of the Word planted."

The condition of one's heart determines if he or she will listen to what is being said. We see the condition of the hearts of men and women:

- Some people have no desire to hear the Word. They will leave it where they find it. Such people take the wealth of God's Word and trample it over.

- Still other people have a desire to have God's Word. Such people want it until they get to the hard-to-do parts. Then they lay it down as a lost cause.

- Other people are deceived in believing that the Word is simply good to have around. Such people read when they can and they have good intentions to spend more time in the Word. But for some reason they always find themselves too busy to read.

- Finally, there are those who delight in God's Word. Such people give themselves totally to its reading and doing. You will read about such people in James 1.

As I listen to Jesus I come to a moment where I see great tragedy (verse 12). There are those who hear Jesus speaking but without interest because their heart places no value in what He is saying. Still others face the same tragedy because they hear but with no heart to change. Such people stay where they are and find the impossibility of being forgiven. Such are the first three groups in the above parable.

As you spend time walking through Scripture and the questions that follow, please consider the condition of your heart as well as the challenge of what to do with the Light that is now in you.

Here are our assignments for the week:

DAY 1:

Read James 1 and answer these questions.
- Why would a person want to read the Bible? Explain.
- How has your life been impacted by listening to the Bible?

DAY 2:

Read Isaiah 55, focusing in on verses 9 and 10. Answer the following questions.
- How can the Bible encourage you each day?
- What has God revealed to you as you have read the Word?

DAY 3:

Read Matthew 13 and answer the following questions.
- What are the purposes of parables?
- What happens when the Word of God is left unopened?

DAY 4:

Read Luke 8 and answer the following questions.
- Explain how the Word becomes a light to your life.
- Explain how you are using the light to reach other people.

DAY 5:

Read Psalm 119 and answer the following questions.
- How can we communicate the Word of God to this present generation?
- How important is the Word of God in the growth of the local church?

WEEK NINE

The Bigger Picture

Scripture focus: Mark 4:26-34

*A*nd he said, "The kingdom of God is as if a man should scatter seed on the ground. He sleeps and rises night and day, and the seed sprouts and grows; he knows not how. The earth produces by itself, first the blade, then the ear, then the full grain in the ear. But when the grain is ripe, at once he puts in the sickle, because the harvest has come."

And he said, "With what can we compare the kingdom of God, or what parable shall we use for it? It is like a grain of mustard seed, which, when sown on the ground, is the smallest of all the seeds on earth, yet when it is sown it grows up and becomes larger than all the garden plants and puts out large branches, so that the birds of the air can make nests in its shade."

With many such parables he spoke the word to them, as they were able to hear it. He did not speak to them without a parable, but privately to his own disciples he explained everything.

The work of an apprentice can sometimes be so tedious and time consuming that the apprentice loses sight of the goal or his or her purpose. One can get so locked into the process that it's easy to overlook the big picture. I started to write, "Imagine if…" but I realized that you do not have to "imagine if . . ." because you and I live in a busy world that if not kept in check will push us into the corner of nothings where we just go around and around on the merry-go-round of life.

This week's focus in clearly on the bigger picture of life.

As Jesus worked with the original set of apprentices, we see them in a "listen moment." Keep in mind that they were being led by the Son of God, who often gave them on-the-job training. The reality is that they were learning "on the fly."

Take a moment and picture them in your mind. They were listening and learning, and eventually they would become the leaders of the church. But here they were trying to get used to a different type of life, a bigger-picture life.

Jesus identifies this life in two parables, which reveal the bigger picture of the kingdom of God.

Question: "What is the kingdom of God?"

We know from studying the gospels that this question is used 108 times. Here is the breakdown of how it is used: "The kingdom of heaven," "God," "the Kingdom come," "the gospel of the Kingdom," "His kingdom," "the kingdom of the Father," "kingdom before the foundation of the world," "Father's kingdom," and "no end to the Kingdom."

There is one more use of this phrase that I now place before you. Jesus said, "My kingdom is not of this world" (John 18:36).

Go back with me to what you have pictured in your mind. The apprentices are hard at work. They are learning as they go. In their minds they are building an earthly kingdom. But Jesus had something else in mind.

He was proclaiming a different message and was providing the way for the apprentices to become members of that kingdom. He also was preparing a movement called the church (Matthew 24:14). The miracle of this message was "this kingdom would have no end."

The two parables before us point us to both our labor in the Kingdom as well as the longevity of the Kingdom. Here is what the parables help us understand about both:

- We are people who labor at sowing seed so people can know about the kingdom of God.

- We are people who see the amazing birth of the seed in people who come to Jesus in salvation.

- We sometimes think our contribution is small. But the seed grows into a mighty kingdom.

- We are the people who will live together forever in that kingdom,

I want to challenge you to think deeply and honestly about whether your life is focused on the bigger picture. I pray that it is. Enjoy this week of study in the kingdom of God.

Here are our assignments for the week:

DAY 1:
Read Psalm 145 and answer the following questions.
- How would you describe God's kingdom work in your life? Give examples.
- How has God made himself known in each generation?

DAY 2:

Read Luke 12 and answer the following questions.

- When will God's kingdom become the kingdom of this world? Cite other scriptures in your answer.
- How does the reality of the coming kingdom affect your future?

DAY 3:

Read John 18 and answer the following questions.

- What does Jesus mean by "My kingdom is not of this world"?
- How should we live as citizens of another country?

DAY 4:

Read Psalm 78 and answer the following questions.

- Why did Israel fail to understand the kingdom of God?
- What excites you most about the coming kingdom of God?

DAY 5:

Read Hebrews 12 and answer the following questions.

- What are some distinguishing characteristics of the kingdom of God?
- What assurances do we have in this life because of the kingdom of God?

WEEK TEN

The First Life Test

Scripture focus: Mark 4:35-41

*O**n that day, when evening had come, he said to them, "Let us go across to the other side." And leaving the crowd, they took him with them in the boat, just as he was. And other boats were with him. And a great windstorm arose, and the waves were breaking into the boat, so that the boat was already filling. But he was in the stern, asleep on the cushion. And they woke him and said to him, "Teacher, do you not care that we are perishing?" And he awoke and rebuked the wind and said to the sea, "Peace! Be still!" And the wind ceased, and there was a great calm. He said to them, "Why are you so afraid? Have you still no faith?" And they were filled with great fear and said to one another, "Who then is this, that even the wind and the sea obey him?"*

Mark 4 begins with Jesus directing His apprentices to listen. Mark 4 ends with the first life test. This test would reveal to the apprentices how much they had grasped in their time with Jesus.

I imagine as Jesus said, "Let's go to the other side," the apprentices were very excited about their day. I wonder, Was pride entering their hearts? In this moment I'm reminded of James MacDonald's definition of trials: "painful circumstances allowed by God in order to transform our conduct and character."

This moment is edged in my memory as a reminder of the need to have faith in the storm. Here is how this test would take place:

- Jesus gives the apprentices a charted course.

He says, "Let us go to the other side." Luke's parallel passage records the following words: "They set out." This kind of sounds like the theme song for Gilligan's Island: "[They] set sail that day for a three-hour tour."

As they sailed it seemed as if everything were right in line. Jesus even fell off to sleep. But then the course changed. A great windstorm came up. The storm was so intense that the Bible says, "The waves were breaking into the boat." The word breaking speaks about the rod of God's correction or the hand of God in a test. God put His hand in the water and stirred up a test.

Immediately we discover how little these men knew about Jesus. We see that they had not progressed in faith. Yes, in the eyes of men they were in danger (Luke 8:23). But the One who was with them would see them through.

- Jesus gives the apprentices a clear guarantee.

We will go over to the other side. God's promises come with His personal guarantee. Hebrews 13:7 speaks about His continual presence with us.

- Jesus works miracles despite our lack of faith.

Jesus arose from His sleep and calmed the storm. It was with a heart of fear that the apprentices asked, "Do you not care?" Jesus had proven He cared by coming to this earth. He would continue to prove His love by going to the Cross (John 3:16). I cannot even imagine the silence in the boat when the storm had ceased.

- Jesus reveals the progress of their faith.

Jesus already knew where they were in faith, and He was now revealing to them where they were. They did not understand the depths of Jesus' love for them. They did not expect a test this early on. They still had not grasped the depths of who He was, but they would in time.

Take time this week as you read and interact with the Scriptures to consider the tests you are presently facing. Embrace them, knowing that God is equipping you for something amazing.

Here are our assignments for the week:

DAY 1:

Read Matthew 8 and answer the following questions.

- With so many miracles happening before the apprentices, one would think they would have faith. What blocked their faith?
- With all the miracles around us, how do *we* lose sight of faith?

DAY 2:

Read 1 Peter 5 and answer the following questions.

- Why is it so hard to place all our storms in God's hands?
- Why does the devil oppose the believer if he knows he
- cannot win?

DAY 3:

Read Psalm 32 and answer the following questions.

- What was David's storm in Psalm 32?
- What types of storms are your close friends going through? List ways you can help them.

DAY 4:

Read James 2 and answer the following questions.

- How does testing build your faith?
- How do faith and works combine to deepen your walk with God?

DAY 5:

Read John 21 and answer the following questions.

- How does God use a failing grade to grow our faith?
- What did Peter learn from his failing grade?

WEEK ELEVEN

What's on the Other Side?

Scripture focus: Mark 5:1-20

They came to the other side of the sea, to the country of the Gerasenes. And when Jesus had stepped out of the boat, immediately there met him out of the tombs a man with an unclean spirit. He lived among the tombs. And no one could bind him anymore, not even with a chain, for he had often been bound with shackles and chains, but he wrenched the chains apart, and he broke the shackles in pieces. No one had the strength to subdue him. Night and day among the tombs and on the mountains he was always crying out and cutting himself with stones. And when he saw Jesus from afar, he ran and fell down before him. And crying out with a loud voice, he said, "What have you to do with me, Jesus, Son of the Most High God? I adjure you by God, do not torment me." For he was saying to him, "Come out of the man, you unclean spirit!" And Jesus asked him, "What is your name?" He replied, "My name is Legion, for we are many." And he begged him earnestly not to send them out of the country. Now a great herd of pigs was feeding there on the hillside, and they begged him, saying, "Send us to the pigs; let us enter them." So he gave them permission. And the unclean spirits came out and entered the pigs; and the herd, numbering about two thousand, rushed down the steep bank into the sea and drowned in the sea.

The herdsmen fled and told it in the city and in the country. And people came to see what it was that had happened. And they came to Jesus and saw the demon-possessed man, the one who had had the legion, sitting there, clothed and in his right mind, and they were afraid. And those who had seen it described to them what had happened to the demon-possessed man and to the pigs. And they began to beg Jesus to depart from their region. As he was getting into the boat, the man who had been possessed with demons begged him that he might be with him. And he did not permit him but said to him, "Go home to your friends and tell them how much the Lord has done for you, and how he has had mercy on you." And he went away and began to proclaim in the Decapolis how much Jesus had done for him, and everyone marveled.

The first lesson of faith was now over. The apprentices were without a doubt very quiet. I wonder if they were thinking, I wonder what's on the other side.

One of the early lessons the apprentice must learn is this: *The leader sets the daily agenda for the apprentice.* This has always been the case. The writer of Proverbs puts it this way in 19:21

> *Many are the plans in the mind of a man,*
> *but it is the purpose of the LORD that will stand.*

Each day our Lord has a plan for our lives, often referred to as "God's will." Have you ever said you would do something if it's the Lord's will? This week we will seek to discover not only how to know God's will but also how to do God's will.

We must keep the following in mind as we read Mark's gospel: Jesus is following His heavenly Father's timeline. Jesus lived to do the

Father's will. This is cool. When the apprentices heard Jesus say, "Let's go to the other side," they knew this was God's will!

Take time to read Mark 5 with this viewpoint. The apprentices were going to step out of the boat fully following Jesus, who is fully in the will of God. They did not know what was on the other side, but God did, and He had a purpose for their going to the other side.

Notice Mark's focus: Jesus stepped out of the boat. The focus is on Jesus. Here is our Messiah leading the apprentices. Immediately they met a man who was in a miserable place. In Luke's account, 8:26-39, we discover how miserable it was for this man. He was possessed by something that had turned his life upside down. He had been forced from a normal life. The people who knew him had no answer for what possessed him. Their feeble attempts only worsened the circumstances. So terrible was the possession that this man was living at the local cemetery. He could be seen running naked and screaming out in pain because of what possessed him.

Think about all that waits for you on the other side of this day. So many people are possessed by things that cause them to lash out at you without even understanding the true issues before them. We are called to walk in the will of God to reach them, because this is God's plan.

Notice how the Messiah took charge of what possessed this man. The demons tried with no avail to overpower Jesus by saying that they were not under His power. But they were under His power (see James 2:10-11). When the demons could not overpower Him, they attempted to avoid His judgment. But they found no home in the pigs. The pigs knew better than to be possessed by demons.

In this moment I look at the apprentices. I see guys who had to be thinking, "I didn't have this on my schedule today." But surely they were coming to understand how God had greater things planned for them than they could imagine (see Jeremiah 29:11).

Brothers and sisters, consider what God has planned for you this week. There are miracles ahead hidden in the mess of problems. You must claim faith in God's will and reject the fear of the mess.

For a second, look at the crowd who had now gathered. They were a mixed-up people who asked the Messiah to leave because they were perfectly happy with their mess. We truly live in a mixed-up world. Let's turn our attention away from such people. Look at the man who had experienced a miracle.

The present has now overcome the past. He is now right side up with a mind that can make decisions that will benefit his life. His desire is to leave the cemetery and follow Christ. Here is a man who believes God's plan is for him to be wherever he is.

In this moment the man hears God's will for his life: "Go home and tell the world what God has done for you." Wow--could it be this simple? Imagine how miraculous our days would be if we simply did God's will.

As you read this week, take small steps and then big steps by going to the other side. God has much for you on the other side. Even now pause and pray, "Lord, carry me to the other side."

Here are our assignments for the week:

DAY 1:
Read Proverbs 16 and answer the following questions.
- How does a believer determine God's daily plan for his or her life?
- What are the dangers of living each day without a plan?

DAY 2:
Read James 4 and answer the following questions.
- According to James, how do we combat the attacks of the enemy?
- According to James, why is it foolish to try to play God?

DAY 3:

Read John 17 and answer the following questions.
- What was God's eternal plan for Jesus?
- What are God's plans for each generation of believers?

DAY 4:

Read Jeremiah 29 and answer the following questions.
- According to Jeremiah, what were the people to spend their days accomplishing while in captivity?
- Where are God's future plans for your life?

DAY 5:

Read Genesis 22 and answer the following questions.
- If you were in Abraham's place, how would you have responded to God's command?
- What type of love did Abraham possess for God, and what type of faith do you possess for God?

WEEK TWELVE

Taking It All In

Scripture focus: Mark 5:21-42

*A*nd when Jesus had crossed again in the boat to the other side, a great crowd gathered about him, and he was beside the sea. Then came one of the rulers of the synagogue, Jairus by name, and seeing him, he fell at his feet and implored him earnestly, saying, "My little daughter is at the point of death. Come and lay your hands on her, so that she may be made well and live." And he went with him.

And a great crowd followed him and thronged about him. And there was a woman who had had a discharge of blood for twelve years, and who had suffered much under many physicians, and had spent all that she had, and was no better but rather grew worse. She had heard the reports about Jesus and came up behind him in the crowd and touched his garment. For she said, "If I touch even his garments, I will be made well." And immediately the flow of blood dried up, and she felt in her body that she was healed of her disease. And Jesus, perceiving in himself that power had gone out from him, immediately turned about in the crowd and said, "Who touched my garments?" And his disciples said to him, "You see the crowd pressing around you, and yet you say, 'Who touched me?'" And he looked around *to see who had done it. But the woman, knowing what had happened to her, came in fear and trembling and fell down before him and told him the whole truth. And he said to her, "Daughter, your faith has made you well; go in peace, and be healed of your disease."*

While he was still speaking, there came from the ruler's house some who said, "Your daughter is dead. Why trouble the Teacher any further?" But overhearing what they said, Jesus said to the ruler of the synagogue, "Do not fear, only believe." And he allowed no one to follow him except Peter and James and John the brother of James. They came to the house of the ruler of the synagogue, and Jesus saw a commotion, people weeping and wailing loudly. And when he had entered, he said to them, "Why are you making a commotion and weeping? The child is not dead but sleeping." And they laughed at him. But he put them all outside and took the child's father and mother and those who were with him and went in where the child was. Taking her by the hand he said to her, "Talitha cumi," which means, "Little girl, I say to you, arise." And immediately the girl got up and began walking (for she was twelve years of age), and they were immediately overcome with amazement.

When we last left the apprentices they were standing at the house of Jairus's daughter, who had just been raised from the dead. Yes, you read it correctly: Jairus's daughter had died. Jesus had indeed raised her from the dead.

In Mark's narrative Jesus leads His apprentices back into the boat. We do not know if He stayed for a few hours or a few days. We just know this group of apprentices were extremely busy. I cannot imagine what they were thinking as they hoisted the sail, grabbed oars, and began paddling back across the lake. Did they talk with Jesus, or was it simply a time to take it all in?

Here is a twenty-first-century apprentice fact: our lives are filled with busyness. Because of this fact, it is important that we train ourselves to take in everything Jesus says. As these men crossed to the other side, more ministry awaited.

A great crowd was waiting for them. They had to meet the needs of the crowd. Ministry can be so demanding on our spiritual minds.

The Bible records the story of a ruler who speaks out in the crowd. Here is a man who has a daughter who is at death's door. He comes believing Jesus can do something about his daughter's problem.

Question: Who was this guy to think that his daughter's needs were more pressing than the totality of the crowd who had gathered? His plea was urgent. The apprentices are taking it all in. What would Jesus do? The Bible says, "He went with him."

Take it in: God cares about the needs of every individual person. Jesus is always available to help those who are in need. Spend some time this week taking in the voices and hurt of those crying for help. What is God asking you to do?

As they were going with the multitudes around Jesus we see him stopping and asking a ridiculous question: "Who touched me?" Take this in: everyone was pushing up against Him. All kinds of people were touching Him. But there was one touch that was different. Someone in the crowd had heard the news about Jesus, and this someone believed He was God. She reached out in faith and was healed.

Jesus wanted her to own her faith and witness her faith so that others would be encouraged to have faith as well. In this moment the news comes--the daughter has died. In this moment I find myself inwardly crying out, "Take it all, in Jairus! Don't give up--the God who conquered disease will conquer death."

What happens next is worth dwelling on. Jesus arrives at the house, where mourners have gathered doing what mourners do. The crowd sees Jesus and begins laughing when Jesus makes a bold statement. Please take it all in: "Do not fear, only believe."

The Bible says Jesus did not allow the doubters to enter the room. Luke records that James, John, and Peter went in with Jesus. In that room the apprentices were about to take in Jesus raising the dead. This is an amazing moment in their lives and in the story of the gospel. In this moment the disciples would get their first taste of Jesus' resurrection power.

Knowing that we have Jesus' resurrection power changes everything for me. I will not stick my head in the sand and say, "I don't hear the cries of the hurting." I will reach out. I will not be afraid of what the enemy throws my way. I have Jesus' resurrection power. I will be available for God's assignments. Nothing is impossible with God.

Take time as you read this week to take it all in!

Here are our assignments for the week:

DAY 1:
Read Hebrews 11 and answer the following questions.
- What do all the people mentioned in Hebrews 11 have in common?
- What type of faith do you need for your life at this moment?

DAY 2:
Read Romans 4 and answer the following questions.
- What did Abraham believe about God?
- What is the New Testament believer's connection with Abraham?

DAY 3:
Read John 3 and answer the following questions.
- "Nick" came at night to see Jesus. Why did he not come in the daytime?
- Why does God want us to live our lives in the light?

DAY 4:

Read 2 Corinthians 1 and answer the following questions.
- What did Paul believe about the purpose of God's comfort in our lives?
- What type of prayer should we be offering for those who are hurting?

DAY 5:

Read 2 Timothy 1 and answer the following questions.
- How could faith in Jesus encourage Timothy in his moment of discouragement?
- How important is it for your family to see you walking in confident faith?

WEEK THIRTEEN

Hometown News

Scripture focus: Mark 6:1-6

He went away from there and came to his hometown, and his disciples followed him. And on the Sabbath he began to teach in the synagogue, and many who heard him were astonished, saying, "Where did this man get these things? What is the wisdom given to him? How are such mighty works done by his hands? Is not this the carpenter, the son of Mary and brother of James and Joses and Judas and Simon? And are not his sisters here with us?" And they took offense at him. And Jesus said to them, "A prophet is not without honor, except in his hometown and among his relatives and in his own household." And he could do no mighty work there, except that he laid his hands on a few sick people and healed them. And he marveled because of their unbelief.

And he went about among the villages teaching.

Imagine if everyone in your hometown had the opportunity to write down one memory they had from your childhood. Imagine if they were all published on Facebook! Would anyone besides me need to leave town? The apprentices of Jesus were about to have an experience in their leader's hometown.

I wonder how Jesus must have felt about going back to where he had spent the first thirty years of His life, first as a carpenter's son and then following in the family business. What were the memories Jesus had of this city, and what did He hope to accomplish here?

When I researched the city of Nazareth I discovered how this city was a Galilean town within the territory of Zebulun. The city was situated close to several main trade routes, which made it easy to contact the outside world. Some would have called it a frontier town. Jesus and his earthly father, Joseph, would have easily found work close to home because the capital of Galilee had been destroyed by the Romans who immediately began to rebuild it again. Work would have been done from their home.

However, there was one big negative: the rest of the Jewish people did not care for these people from Nazareth. Therefore, Nathaniel said when he heard about Jesus, "Can anything good come out of Nazareth?"

Christ-followers know that something good did come out of the city! That something was someone--Jesus Christ. Imagine as the crowds who followed and often ran after Jesus came to His hometown with the news "Jesus is coming to town." Did they print "Hometown Boy Returns" or "Hometown Hero Returns"? The Bible does not tell us what they were saying in anticipation of His coming. But it does give us insight once Jesus gets to town.

Mark does not record anything about Jesus' first hours and even days in the city. We don't know if he visited his family or any of his childhood friends. There is no mention of his going to his boyhood home. Mark simply tells us about where Jesus goes on the Sabbath.

At the synagogue Jesus is asked to speak, as is the common courtesy for a visiting rabbi, and most the hometown folk are astonished. The word used by Mark could have a wide range of meanings from being practically challenged to being angry at being challenged. I believe it is the probability that they were thinking, "Who is this hometown boy telling us how to live our lives?"

Notice how they make excuses that would validate why they would not listen to Him. They give his qualifications: "A carpenter's son." He's just a common man. He has no rabbinical training. "He is the Son of Mary." Here they were referring to His having, in their minds, been born out of wedlock. He is the brother of James, Joses, Judas, and Simon. They supposedly know all about him. They even know who his sisters are.

So, they conclude, "He has no authority to speak to us."

Then the natural response would be, according to Mark, to take offense. This means they got fired-up mad.

Notice Jesus' response: "A prophet is without honor . . ." Just like Joseph, Moses, and Jeremiah, Jesus is without respect from His people. So common was this concept that Jewish tradition emphasized this concept even more.

In this moment I pause and imagine the shock on the faces of the apprentices as the people reject the help of the Lord. I see the disbelief as they refuse to even listen to the words of the Son of God. What would you have thought if you had been there?

Mark gives us a footnote in letting us know that few people believed, but the majority were in the unbelief camp. As Jesus leaves the city, I picture Him shaking His head as He was astounded by their unbelief. This is a shock to my system. The word used here by Mark speaks of someone who is an infidel, a person who rejects God.

In this moment I ask myself, Why did God want this in His Word? Ask yourself the same question. Take time this week to work through the answer as you read each day's Scripture readings. Ask yourself about what you want the people in your own hometown to know about you and about Christ.

Here are our assignments for the week:

DAY 1:

Read Matthew 13:34-38 and John 1:43-50, and answer the following questions:.

- What did the people in Nazareth know about Jesus' family, and what do the people in your hometown know about you?
- How difficult is it to share Christ in your own hometown?

DAY 2:

Read Jeremiah 31 and answer the following questions.

- What were the problems in the nation of Israel, and what hope did she have?
- What problems does our nation have, and what hope do we as believers offer?

DAY 3:

Read Jeremiah 32 and answer the following questions.

- Who was to blame for the disasters in Israel?
- Why was Jeremiah willing to go through such mistreatment by his hometown?

DAY 4:

Read Acts 14 and answer the following questions.

- How can success in ministry become a trap when you are sharing the gospel?
- How would you respond to someone who attempted to persecute you or your family?

DAY 5:

Read 1 Timothy 6 and answer the following questions.

- Explain what it means to "fight the good fight of faith."
- Take time to be reminded of who is this Jesus you are following. Write down your observations:

———————— ✕ ————————

WEEK FOURTEEN

The Easter Miracle

Scripture focus: 2 Corinthians 8:9

For you know the grace of our Lord Jesus Christ, that though he was rich, yet for your sake he became poor, so that you by his poverty might become rich.

This week we hit the pause button in our studies in the gospel of Mark. This is Easter week, and it would be tragic to miss out on the glorious truth of this week. Speaking to the church at Corinth, Paul writes the verse listed above, which gripped my heart as I thought about all this week means.

Jesus Christ left the perfection of heaven for you and me. Allow this to sink in. Jesus was in a place of full authority without any assault from the enemy. He was in a place where everything was at His call, but He came here.

Anyone who is an apprentice of Jesus must often call himself or herself back to the reminder of all Jesus gave for us. If we fail to do this, we will become disenchanted with all we face as His followers.

Think for a moment where we were with Jesus just last week. We were back in His earthly hometown. This was where He grew to manhood. It was here where He worked with His father in the carpentry business. It was here where He would come to His father after completing a project with the awesome pronouncement: "Finished."

The people in His hometown rejected Him as the Messiah. They refused to believe He was God. So the sad reality was that they remained in spiritual poverty even though spiritual riches were offered to them.

Fast forward with me to Good Friday, the day when Jesus willingly went to the cross. There we see Him hanging on the Cross. Seconds before He surrenders His life into the Father's safekeeping, He says one word, as noted in the Greek New Testament, "Τετε λεσται." Our translations say, "It is finished" (John 19:30).

Jesus has now completed the task of purchasing our forgiveness on the Cross. He has become the payment for our sins (Romans 3:25). He cries out the words of an Easter miracle, "Finished." Jesus' cry is a victory cry.

As you consider your life this Easter week, do you find yourself in need of an Easter miracle? Chances are that most who read this have some circumstance that requires a miracle.

As I write this devotion I am sitting in the dentist's office with Sherry. I look around to see all the people who each seem to be locked in their own world of needs. I think, "Lord, how many of these people even know that You are the source of all miracles?"

I turn my attention back to God's Word and ask myself, "Did Jesus want to be on the Cross?" I know this seems like a heretical question, but according to Scripture it is not. Hebrews 12:3 speaks of the joy that was before Him. Isaiah 53:10-13 speaks of the joy He would have in knowing the result of His sacrifice on the Cross.

Brothers and sisters, Easter was and still is full of miracles. This week in these devotionals you will interact with five people who needed an Easter miracle. It is my prayer that you would place your needs before the Lord as you spend this week in God's Word.

Here are our assignments for the week:

DAY 1:

Read Matthew 27:15-26 and answer the following questions.

- If you could give anyone an Easter miracle, who would it be and why would you give it?
- What must it have felt like for Barabbas to have faced both certain death and to have experienced unmerited grace?

DAY 2:

Read John 21 and answer the following questions.

- How many of the disciples needed God's forgiveness? Explain your answer.
- Describe the moment when Peter saw and recognized Jesus. Write down this same moment in your life.

DAY 3:

Read John 20:24-29 and answer the following questions.

- What is the toughest part of having to wait for a miracle? Explain.
- Why did Thomas have such a hard time believing in the resurrection of Jesus?

DAY 4:

Read John 20:1-18 and answer the following questions.

- Describe the hurt these women must have been facing as they came to the tomb of Jesus.

- Why did Mary Magdalene wait at the tomb of Jesus when the others left?

DAY 5:

Read Romans 6 and answer the following questions.
- How many people are afraid of death? Explain.
- What does Jesus' resurrection mean for you personally?

WEEK FIFTEEN

It's Your Turn Now

Scripture focus: Mark 6:7-13

And he called the twelve and began to send them out two by two, and gave them authority over the unclean spirits. He charged them to take nothing for their journey except a staff—no bread, no bag, no money in their belts—but to wear sandals and not put on two tunics. And he said to them, "Whenever you enter a house, stay there until you depart from there. And if any place will not receive you and they will not listen to you, when you leave, shake off the dust that is on your feet as a testimony against them." So they went out and proclaimed that people should repent. And they cast out many demons and anointed with oil many who were sick and healed them.

Several years ago I sat in my living room and watched as a son told the story of how for many years his dad had tried to prepare him to lead the family business. Week after week and sadly year after year the son paid very little attention to what his dad was trying to teach him. But it all changed when his dad suddenly died.

The son said, "Suddenly I was thrust into leadership, and I realized I had not paid attention to all that Dad was trying to teach me."

Last year I was talking with one of our younger church leaders who was feeling a bit useless to a team he was a part of and was considering stepping out of the group. Here was my response: "Do you realize that a lot of the people on the team are getting older? There's coming a time when you and I will have to lead the team." In that moment the person's entire viewpoint was changed as he realized that it would soon be his turn.

As Jesus continued to minister in the villages (Mark 6:6), the apprentices were probably clueless as to what was about to take place. Jesus called the twelve guys (you can see their names in Matthew 10:2-4) and said, "It's your turn now."

Jesus was going to send them out to carry out and extend the ministry. The heading in my Bible reads, "Jesus sends out the twelve Apostles." R. C. Sproul writes, "The words 'send them out' have the same root as the noun apostle. Both underline their link with Jesus. They are His personal representatives" (Reformation Study Bible, 1423).

This is important business for the church. These guys would become the appointed leaders in with office of apostle. All that the church would be told about Jesus would come through (at the beginning) these men.

This had to have been scary and the most serious moment of their ministry to date. There was without doubt spiritual warfare going on. These men were called to be what you and I are called to be: ambassadors of Christ (2 Corinthians 5:20).

I remember being in a training class in North Carolina with a group of people who we were training to go out on visitation. One of those people on our team was a very successful business person. All week long I noticed this person's uneasiness. On the night when we were to go out to share what we had learned, she went into the bathroom and threw up in agony and fear. This woman understood the seriousness of souls hanging in the balance. She did not want to mess it up.

I think this is a good point at which to insert this question: "Have you responded to the call to represent Jesus in the world?" Studies show that ninety-five percent of all believers never share their faith. This is a serious issue in our day.

Notice how Jesus prepared them for the moment when they were to go out:

- He directed them to go, two by two.

This was for a dual purpose. One was for support. The Bible tells us that Jesus never leaves us alone (Hebrews 13:6). The other was for validation and accountability. In Matthew 18:16 Jesus says that a witness is established by two witnesses.

- He directs them to go with the clothes on their back.

Jesus was teaching them about the importance of trusting Him for their daily need. We must also trust God to provide what we need in His word (Philippians 4:19).

- He directs them to walk through the open doors He would provide for them.

God promises that His Word will never return void. God promises us success in the gospel (Philippians 1:6).

- He directs them to shake off the dust of their feet when rejected.

In the Old Testament the people of Israel would always shake the dust off their feet when they came out of a Gentile area and return to their homeland, signifying shaking off the practices of the heathen. It symbolized that when people rejected God, God rejected them.

Now we see the guys pairing in teams of two, and off they go. Before long they would return with the amazing news of how God extended the Kingdom through their work.

An important question to ask yourself is "Am I ready to go and share the gospel?" What it the elders of your church suddenly died or were called away; would you be ready to lead? I want to challenge you as you read this week's selected scriptures to closely take in what you are reading, because it could be your time now.

Here are our assignments for the week:

DAY 1:
Read Philippians 4 and answer the following questions.
- How difficult is it to trust God with leading your life?
- What would be the toughest place for you to be God's representative? Explain.

DAY 2:
Read 2 Timothy 4 and answer the following questions.
- What was Timothy's toughest assignment as a pastor?
- Did Paul regret being a representative of Jesus? Explain.

DAY 3:
Read Luke 10 and answer the following questions:
- Have you ever given up on some one? Explain.
- How many people in your church do you believe are praying about their children becoming harvesters for Jesus? Explain.

DAY 4:
Read Ephesians 6 and answer the following questions.
- How important is it for the follower of Jesus to wear all the armor of God?
- Describe each piece of God's armor.

DAY 5:

Read Isaiah 1 and answer the following questions.

- Was Isaiah's mission field a difficult place? Explain.
- What did the Lord want Isaiah to tell these people?

WEEK SIXTEEN

The Herod Syndrome

Scripture focus: Mark 6:14-28

King Herod heard of it, for Jesus' name had become known. Some said, "John the Baptist has been raised from the dead. That is why these miraculous powers are at work in him." But others said, "He is Elijah." And others said, "He is a prophet, like one of the prophets of old." But when Herod heard of it, he said, "John, whom I beheaded, has been raised." For it was Herod who had sent and seized John and bound him in prison for the sake of Herodias, his brother Philip's wife, because he had married her. For John had been saying to Herod, "It is not lawful for you to have your brother's wife." And Herodias had a grudge against him and wanted to put him to death. But she could not, for Herod feared John, knowing that he was a righteous and holy man, and he kept him safe. When he heard him, he was greatly perplexed, and yet he heard him gladly.

But an opportunity came when Herod on his birthday gave a banquet for his nobles and military commanders and the leading men of Galilee. For when Herodias's daughter came in and danced, she pleased Herod and his guests. And the king said to the girl, "Ask me for whatever you wish, and I will give it to you." And he vowed to her, "Whatever you ask me, I will give you, up to half of my kingdom." And she went out and said to her mother, "For what should I ask?" And she said, "The head of John the Baptist." And she came in immediately with haste to the king and asked, saying, "I want you to give me at once the head of John the Baptist on a platter." And the king was exceedingly sorry, but because of his oaths and his guests he did not want to break his word to her. And immediately the king sent an executioner with orders to bring John's head. He went and beheaded him in the prison and brought his head on a platter and gave it to the girl, and the girl gave it to her mother.

This week's Scripture focus puts us in a difficult place. As the apprentices are following Jesus, the news comes that John the Baptist is dead. I can hear Peter asking, "How did it happen? Was it a heart attack--or was it Herod's doing?"

So much of what happens around us is heard about in the vacuum of making observations based upon what we think or what someone else has said without really knowing the facts. Here are the facts about this situation:

- John the Baptist had known from childhood that the greatest event of the age was at hand, the coming of the Messiah, and that he, John, was to be the one to tell people He was coming (Malachi 3:1; 4:5).

- John's message was simple: "Repent." Those who responded to his message were to be baptized in anticipation of the Messiah's coming.

- Halley comments, "At the height of his popularity, he baptized Jesus and proclaimed Him to be the Messiah. Then, when his mission was accomplished, he passed off the scene" (*Halley's Bible Handbook*, 654).

- John would continue preaching for a few months and would get caught in the Herod syndrome.

You ask, "What is the Herod syndrome?" Hold your question-- I promise we'll get to the answer soon.

In Jesus' day Rome was the conquering nation of the world. All of Palestine was under the rule of Rome. To be able to control the region, Rome used political along with military might to keep the world under her thumb. One of those political leaders was Herod, who was given the title as king of the region.

He was very much a wicked man. In Mark's account we discover one aspect of his depraved life. He took his niece, who was married to his half-brother Phillip, convincing her to divorce Phillip and to marry him.

Herod has himself in a place where his life is morally spinning out of control. In this moment of Jesus' ministry Herod has heard about all that is going on in Jesus' ministry. John MacArthur comments, "He was greatly alarmed when he received the news about Jesus. He thinks John the Baptist has returned from the dead."

You and I would ask, "Why was Herod concerning himself with John the Baptist?" Mark answers that question in this week's Scripture focus. Take time to read the story and consider the implications of living a life that is morally out of control. This is the Herod syndrome.

As you read you will see no fewer than four indicators of this syndrome:

1. A person who cannot grasp the truth of God

When Herod meets John, probably shortly after Jesus' baptism, he confronts Herod with his sin, which mirrors the depraved life Paul writes about in Romans 1:29.

He liked to hear John, but he could not stand what he was saying now and thus has him thrown into prison. This is what happens when leaders hate the light (John 3:18-29). Most believe John will stay there about sixteen months. It is during this time that even John gets discouraged (Matthew 11).

Each time Herod would hear John, the worse his anger would become. But he would not have him killed because he knew this was a righteous and holy man.

2. A person who cannot get a handle on his or her perversions

He was unwilling to make things right with God and people. He lived on in this sinful relationship. He knew his wife had a grudge against John, and he knew deep inside that this was going to bite him in the end.

He probably thought that arresting John would appease her, but it did not. Here was the perversion surrounding him: his wife was filled with hatred, his step-daughter was seductive, hell oversaw him, and he was totally engrossed in depravity.

God, in kindness, had placed John in his path. However, it was to no avail to the man with such a syndrome.

3. A person who cannot do what is right

In the scene before us a sinful party ends up in a point of no return. Herod backs himself into a corner he cannot get out of. His wife has so turned hate into malice. She would never heed God's warnings (1 Peter 2:1; Colossians 3:8; Titus 3:3). It was a point of no return.

A person who comes to this point ends up living with regret, shame, and a life filled with fear and no peace.

4. A person who dies without hope

John the Baptist loses his head in this syndrome. Halley comments, "John spent thirty years of his life in seclusion, 1½ *years of public preaching, a year and 4 months in prison*--and then the final curtain. But look what he accomplished, He ushered the coming of the Son of God" (Halley's Bible Hand-book, 654).

But what did Jesus say about Him? "There has arisen no one greater than John the Baptist" (Matthew 11:11).

Herod would come to the end of his life a miserable failure. He would stand before God, without hope because he did not know the Messiah.

What will you and I do when we stand before Jesus? For each of us, I trust we will say, "I followed Jesus as my Savior" (see John 1:29).

Here are our assignments for the week:

DAY 1:

Read Malachi 3 and answer the following questions.
- How was John the Baptist the fulfillment of this prophecy?
- How does the believers' call mirror the call of John the Baptist? One hint: It centers around the Second Coming.

DAY 2:

Read I Kings 19 and answer the following questions.
- Why did Elijah suddenly give up?
- Think about how God speaks in tough moments. How is God attempting to get your attention?

DAY 3:

Read Luke 9 and answer the following questions.
- How important was it for Peter to grasp the depths and heights of who Jesus is?
- What was the significance of the "transfiguration?"

DAY 4:

Read I Corinthians 2 and answer the following questions.

- Why is it so difficult for an unbeliever to understand the Scriptures?
- What role does the Spirit play in our reaching the lost?

DAY 5:

Read Romans 1 and answer the following questions.

- How does the world respond to our pointing out sin?
- How does the world deal with resentment?

WEEK SEVENTEEN

Desperate for Answers

Scripture focus: Mark 6:30-42

*T*he apostles returned to Jesus and told him all that they had done and taught. And he said to them, "Come away by yourselves to a desolate place and rest a while." For many were coming and going, and they had no leisure even to eat. And they went away in the boat to a desolate place by themselves. Now many saw them going and recognized them, and they ran there on foot from all the towns and got there ahead of them. When he went ashore he saw a great crowd, and he had compassion on them, because they were like sheep without a shepherd. And he began to teach them many things. And when it grew late, his disciples came to him and said, "This is a desolate place, and the hour is now late. Send them away to go into the surrounding countryside and villages and buy themselves something to eat." But he answered them, "You give them something to eat." And they said to him, "Shall we go and buy two hundred denarii worth of bread and give it to them to eat?" And he said to them, "How many loaves do you have? Go and see." And when they had found out, they said, "Five, and two fish." Then he commanded them all to sit down in groups on the green grass. So they sat down in groups, by hundreds and by fifties. And taking *the five loaves and the two fish, he looked up to heaven and said a blessing and broke the loaves and gave them to the disciples to set before the people. And he divided the two fish among them all. And they all ate and were satisfied.*

When we last looked at our Scripture focus the disciples of John the Baptist were laying to rest the headless body of John the Baptist. The verses before us connect back to chapter 6, verses 7-13. The apprentices were being sent out to do ministry. Please refer to week 15 in our devotions to familiarize yourself with where this week's scripture picks up.

The apprentices return from their ministry tour all cranked because of what has happened. But at the same time Jesus sees the fatigue. He calls them to come away for a moment of rest and reflection. He simply says, "You need rest." Can anyone identify with this?

They get in the boat to go to a desolate place (a place with few people). But once they arrive, the people have anticipated where they were going and have gotten there faster than they did. It's kind of like the plague finding you wherever you are.

Jesus has a different approach. He sees them as they are, "sheep without a shepherd." This is the way it always is with those who are true shepherds (1 Peter 5:1-4).

Jesus spends the entire day teaching in spite of being exhausted. Here is where things take a turn that you and I would be familiar with. The apprentices come and say, "It's enough, Lord. We've done enough. It's time that they go." Has anyone besides me ever made such statements?

Jesus, if we keep them any longer we're going to have a mess on our hands.

Question: Are you in a moment when a decision has to be made? Or maybe you're in a moment when you're convinced you have the answer and it is the best decision in this moment.

Question: Have you asked Jesus or have you listened to Jesus? Jesus' response to the apprentices leads us to believe that they had not sought His wisdom. The God of compassion challenges the apprentices to do something about this desperate moment.

In John's account (6:7) we gain insight. Jesus was testing them. When God tests us, do we make decisions that have human answers, decisions that are void of faith or expectations or are miracle-free?

The apprentices access the situation and come up with the best answer: "Send them away--there is nothing that can be done." But wait--Jesus is here! The apprentices are looking at their resources. There are only five small muffins and two small sardines.

These guys had no time, no resources, no heart, or no stomach for a miracle. But one kid must have. He apparently knew that nothing is impossible in Jesus' hands!

This is the truth we need in desperate moments. Take time this week to read each day's readings with a heart to understand the depths of this truth. After reading each day's assignments, I challenge you to make three applications:

1. Place your *moments* in God's hands
   (Matthew 6:25-34).

2. Place your *mountains* in God's hands
   (Mark 9:23-24).

3. Place your *miseries* in God's hands
   (1 Peter 5:6-7).

After you have made application, wait for the miracle. It is surely coming down that dusty road!

Here are our assignments for the week:

DAY 1:

Read Genesis 18 and answer the following questions:

- Consider Abraham and Sarah. How desperate would you have been if you were in their situation?
- Consider the judgment that was coming. How bold would you have been before the Lord?

DAY 2:

Read Matthew 14 and answer the following questions.

- What types of struggles did the apprentices face in this chapter?
- How would you have responded if you had seen Jesus walking on the water?

DAY 3:

Read Philippians 4 and answer the following questions.

- Why does prayer sometimes seem so insufficient when we are searching for answers?
- How does Philippians 4:13 apply when we need answers?

DAY 4:

Read 2 Corinthians 1 and answer the following questions.

- How much mercy does God offer each of us in the difficult moments of life?
- What are we to do with the lessons we learn in the desperate moments of life?

DAY 5:

Read John 6 and answer the following questions.

- Why did the people want to take Jesus by force?
- Why do we want Jesus in the boat of our desperation?

WEEK EIGHTEEN

Not So Fast

Scripture focus: Mark 6:45-52

*I*mmediately Jesus made His disciples get into the boat and go ahead of Him to the other side to Bethsaida, while He Himself was sending the crowd away. After bidding them farewell, He left for the mountain to pray.

When it was evening, the boat was in the middle of the sea, and He was alone on the land. Seeing them straining at the oars, for the wind was against them, at about the fourth watch of the night He came to them, walking on the sea; and He intended to pass by them. But when they saw Him walking on the sea, they supposed that it was a ghost, and cried out; for they all saw Him and were terrified. But immediately He spoke with them and said to them, "Take courage; it is I, do not be afraid." Then He got into the boat with them, and the wind stopped; and they were utterly astonished, for they had not gained any insight from the incident of the loaves, but their heart was hardened (NASB).

As we continue to journey along with the other apprentices of Jesus, we come to a moment that Mark introduces with a simple word: immediately. This word grabs my attention as I consider the miracle that has just taken place.

Has Jesus taken a spiritual needle and popped the spiritual balloons of each of His apprentices? Has our Lord become a "Debbie Downer?" The answer is clearly "No!" There is something deeper at work here that demands our immediate attention, a shaking of our spiritual direction.

When I read the word immediately I think about the phrase "Not so fast." This phrase comes from the lips of ESPN's College Game Day analysist Lee Corso, who for the last twenty years has used it each time he has disagreed with the other analysist's game day picks. His goal is to show him the obvious viewpoint on the other side of the coin.

Here in Mark 6 Jesus has a different opinion as to what was taking place. In one of our readings for this week, John 6:16-21, we will dig deep into what was happening. Let me simply say here that the crowds had come to believe that it was time for Jesus to set up His earthly kingdom and for the apprentices to be in His government. In the eyes of the apprentices this was awesome. It was the time, and they believed they had the talent.

Hear the words of Jesus--"Not so fast." If He were to take this detour, the Cross would no longer be in His future. If He were to take this detour, our eternal destiny would be hell. If He were to take this detour, the plan of God for our redemption would remain incomplete. If Jesus were to take this detour, it would prove that He had not come as God to be the Savior of the world. In this moment I find myself saying to the apprentices, "Not so fast!"

Take time this week to consider how our Lord puts everything into perspective. He immediately moves these men away from the detour.

He places them into a boat and sends them out as He goes before the Father to pray for them. In the middle of the night it becomes clear that these apprentices are not ready to rule the world. They cannot even rule a storm. Jesus, as only He can, comes in the early hours of the morning walking in the very storm that was breaking down the false confidence these apprentices were plagued with.

As we see Jesus walking on the water, we see grace at work. Jesus allows Peter to get out of the boat. It was a moment of strengthening of Peter's faith as well as a moment of humbling his faith. Peter would cry out three amazing grace words, "Lord, save me!"

As the waves tried to take Peter, I hear those same words in my mind--"Not so fast." Jesus reaches out and takes Peter by the hand, places him into the boat, and speaks to the storm. In a moment the sea is at peace and the disciples are at peace.

Brother and sisters, you and I need the "not so fast" moments to bring us to a place of walking in God's sovereign plan. Here are some "not so fast" reminders:

- We are all sunk in this life without Jesus' grace.

- We can each cry out to Jesus because He is a God of grace.

- We each have those moments when we fail to seek grace.

- We each need storms to remind us of who is really in charge.

Take time this week to discover God's "not so fast" messages in your life.

Here are our assignments for the week:

DAY 1:

Read Romans 12 and answer the following questions.

- Does your life sometimes look like a combination of shared leadership? Explain your thoughts:
- How difficult is life when you are trying to fight God for the leadership in your life?

DAY 2:

Read Psalm 37 and answer the following questions.

- What was the storm in David's life?
- How comforting is it to know that God is for you? Explain.

DAY 3:

Read Acts 27 and answer the following questions.

- Did Paul have any fears in his life?
- Would you have found it easy to believe Paul if you had been in the boat with him? Explain.

DAY 4:

Read Numbers 14--15 and answer the following questions.

- Why did the people struggle with obeying God? Explain.
- Why was God not going to go with them? Explain.

DAY 5:

Read Exodus 17 and answer the following questions.

- What does God think about our complaints?
- Why did God provide for His people even though they were always filled with complaints? Compare your life to theirs in your answer.

Where are the Men?

Scripture focus: Mark 6:53-56

When they had crossed over they came to land at Gennesaret, and moored to the shore. When they got out of the boat, immediately the people recognized Him, and ran about that whole country and began to carry here and there on their pallets those who were sick, to the place they heard He was. Wherever He entered villages, or cities, or countryside, they were laying the sick in the market places, and imploring Him that they might just touch the fringe of His cloak; and as many as touched it were being cured (NASB).

As I write this chapter I am sitting with the guys who are a part of a mission team in Malawi. Each guy is unique in many ways. One of the guys is bouncing off the wall because he is a morning person. As I look to the left, I see a guy staring at the wall because he is not a morning person. Most of the guys don't realize how unusual they are in comparison to most of the other men of the world. What makes them so unusual is that these men are on mission with God.

As we focus on this week's scripture, it's important that we understand how vital this commentary is. If God placed this in Scripture, it's important. Keep in mind that Mark is writing under the inspiration of Scripture (see 2 Peter 1:20-21). God wanted us to see this and understand what was happening here.

As Jesus ministered, we come to understand how men were on mission with God. According to Matthew 14:34-36, men of the region enthusiastically gathered together all the broken people who they could get to Jesus. Picture these broken people beside the road as Jesus passed by. Picture people as they are crying out, "Have mercy!" while others were reaching out their hands hoping just to touch Him. Finally, see those who could not move but were simply lying there waiting and hoping for the help that only God could give.

Allow the Scripture to open your eyes to ministry. The most important mission known to humanity is the mission to reach broken people. I can almost hear the amens coming from those who read this chapter.

Take a moment and ask yourself, Who were these broken people? Mark simply identifies them as people who were sick. Ask yourself, Who were these men?" Mark simply identifies them as people from the land and region of Gennesaret. Brothers and sisters, God intends for each of us to be willing to serve those who are sick in our midst.

The above statement leads me to another question: Who are the sick in our midst? Here in Zomba, Malawi, the sick are all around us. I saw a man begging as we got water from the local Metro (the Sam's Club of Malawi). I walked by three children who were begging for food or money. We walked through villages where children were sick from enduring malnutrition. Others were sick from drinking dirty water. But their greater need is the gospel, which is the only help for the spiritual sickness they face every day.

As I sit here I imagine Jesus walking these dusty roads. I see Him with eyes of compassion. I see Him with love in His heart for all the people. But I also imagine the sickness of men where I live. I visualize the ones who are sick with cancer, diabetes, heart conditions, paralysis from strokes, extreme arthritis, liver diseases, or dementia. But just as it is in a foreign country, so is it in America—people are spiritually sick.

The men in Mark's account took it personally upon themselves to get the sick people to Jesus. It was their view that Jesus would make a difference—that drove them. They believed Jesus could do what no other man could do. But they also, according to Mark's account, implored Jesus to allow them to touch Him. Literally, they were crying out for Jesus to help.

Wow—this is so awesome to me. Here are men who are committed to giving themselves to reaching sick people. I see each of them in the dusty Galilean countryside visiting someone who was sick. He says, "Jesus is passing by, and I want to take you to see Him." He continues, "When I see Him, I'll cry out for you." This is a man's man, or better put, a God's man!

This has been what the men on our team have been doing this week. They have been going to where spiritually sick people are, and they have pleaded with them to come to Jesus. This was, and is, a great expense to them. But they are willing to give because of the outcome of what they're doing.

This week I pray that you and I will see the need for being people about the business of reaching sick people. Pay close attention to those who were men's men in their day. Also pay close attention to how God would speak to you about your need to serve the sick around you.

Here are our assignments for the week:

DAY 1:

Read Proverbs 14:31 and answer the following questions.

- Who are the poor among us? Identify them and consider how you can personally help them.
- Since there is enough food produced in the world to feed every person, why is there so much poverty in the world? Explain.

DAY 2:

Read Amos 6 and answer the following questions.

- Does our desire for comfort get in the way of caring for those who need our help? Explain.
- What does God have to say to those who exploit the poor? Explain.

DAY 3:

Read 2 Corinthians 8 and answer the following questions.

- How did Jesus identify with the poor of this world? Explain.
- What led to the people's decision to send relief to the poor as noted in 2 Corinthians 8?

DAY 4:

Read Deuteronomy 15:7-11 and answer the following questions.

- Why are some people born poor and others born rich? Give reasons.
- What is God saying to the church about the poor among us?

DAY 5:

Read Luke 12:15-20 and Proverbs 21:13 and answer the following questions.

- Why did the rich man focus only on bettering himself? Explain.
- How effective is your prayer life today?

WEEK TWENTY

Getting to the Heart of the Matter

Scripture focus: Mark 7:1-23

The Pharisees and some of the scribes gathered around Him when they had come from Jerusalem, and had seen that some of His disciples were eating their bread with impure hands, that is, unwashed. (For the Pharisees and all the Jews do not eat unless they carefully wash their hands, thus observing the traditions of the elders; and when they come from the market place, they do not eat unless they cleanse themselves; and there are many other things which they have received in order to observe, such as the washing of cups and pitchers and copper pots.) The Pharisees and the scribes asked Him, "Why do Your disciples not walk according to the tradition of the elders, but eat their bread with impure hands?" And He said to them, "Rightly did Isaiah prophesy of you hypocrites, as it is written:

> *'This people honors Me with their lips,*
> *But their heart is far away from Me.*
> *'But in vain do they worship Me,*
> *Teaching as doctrines the precepts of men.'*

Neglecting the commandment of God, you hold to the tradition of men."

He was also saying to them, "You are experts at setting aside the commandment of God in order to keep your tradition. For Moses said, 'HONOR YOUR FATHER AND YOUR MOTHER'; and, 'HE WHO SPEAKS EVIL OF FATHER OR MOTHER, IS TO BE PUT TO DEATH'; but you say, 'If a man says to his father or his mother, whatever I have that would help you is Corban (that is to say, given to God),' you no longer permit him to do anything for his father or his mother; thus invalidating the word of God by your tradition which you have handed down; and you do many things such as that."

After He called the crowd to Him again, He began saying to them, "Listen to Me, all of you, and understand: there is nothing outside the man which can defile him if it goes into him; but the things which proceed out of the man are what defile the man. [If anyone has ears to hear, let him hear."]

When he had left the crowd and entered the house, His disciples questioned Him about the parable. And He said to them, "Are you so lacking in understanding also? Do you not understand that whatever goes into the man from outside cannot defile him, because it does not go into his heart, but into his stomach, and is eliminated?" (Thus He declared all foods clean.) And He was saying, "That which proceeds out of the man, that is what defiles the man. For from within, out of the heart of men, proceed the evil thoughts, fornications, thefts, murders, adulteries, deeds of coveting and wickedness, as well as deceit, sensuality, envy, slander, pride and foolishness. All these evil things proceed from within and defile the man" (NASB).

As the couple sat down in my office, it was clear they were at a point of deep contention with each other. As I gently probed into their story, I began to hear things like "I'm tired of telling him to replace the toilet paper roll so it rolls downward. He does it on purpose."

In this moment I ask you, How does a person get to the heart of the matter? Now I could have said Bob Newhart's classic line, "Stop it." Or I could have chosen to direct them to compromise, each taking a turn with each new roll to simply do it his or her way.

But the issues of the heart are much deeper. It was the same way in Jesus' day. He said, "Out of the abundance of the heart the mouth speaks" (Matthew 12:34). The truth is—getting to the heart of each matter can be tough work.

Here in Mark 7 we see Jesus' ministry at a level you and I could never possibly describe. Look back to last week's study on Mark 6:53-56. One would think that at this point surely Jesus' ministry would be accepted. But the cold hearts of the religious leaders kept them from seeing Jesus for who He really was.

As I write this devotion I am sitting in the doctor's office with John, who has bronchitis. We're waiting for the doctor to prescribe his treatment. As I sit here looking at Matthew 7, I find myself comparing it to a Billy Graham crusade. Can you imagine as Dr. Graham is giving the invitation that someone steps up to the platform and says, "You guys are going to have to stop coming forward, because I have just discovered that Dr. Graham did not wash his hands before he opened the Bible." Each of us would laugh at this person and call him or her crazy. But the truth is--something is wrong in the person's heart.

Pay close attention to the scene before us. This week you will read five passages that lead you to engage in heart issues. I want to start the process by identifying two statements from Jesus' encounter in Matthew 7.

- The condition of your heart determines the lens through which you and I view life.

Jesus' heart was pure. When He ministered, He liberated those He ministered to. He also could confront those who were either legalistic or filled with worldly ways. The heart is always deceptive when the lens is polluted. Jesus' opponents were people who valued tradition more than truth. Because of this view, they found themselves being ruthless people with their families and with the matters of justice and mercy.

- The choices of your heart reveal the truth of what is in your heart.

Pay close attention to how Jesus and how His opponents conducted themselves in day-to-day life. I truly have come to understand the following:

1. What I say reveals who I am.
2. What I *don't* say reveals who I am.
3. What I do reveals who I am.
4. What I *don't* do reveals who I am.

Only when our hearts have been purified by Jesus can we make right choices, because righteousness then dwells in the heart. Question: "Do you need a heart check-up? Or maybe do you need a heart change?" Jesus is the one who changes hearts. Take time this week to pray daily for God to reveal to you what is in your heart.

Here are our assignments for the week:

DAY 1:

Read 2 Samuel 11 and answer the following questions.

- How could David (a man after God's own heart) commit such a dark sin?
- How could David continue with an unrepentant heart for over one year?

DAY 2:

Read Psalm 32 and Psalm 51 and answer the following questions.

- What changed David's heart? Explain.
- What did David now want to do for others?

DAY 3:

Read Acts 10 and answer the following questions.

- What was the condition of Peter's heart?
- What did God intend for Peter to have in his heart?

DAY 4:

Read Isaiah 29 and answer the following questions.

- What had the teachings of the religious leaders accomplished in the hearts of the people?
- What hope was there for such wicked hearts?

DAY 5:

Read 1 Corinthians 5 and answer the following questions.

- What was the condition of the hearts of the people in the church at Corinth?
- How much sin does it take to destroy the heart?

WEEK TWENTY-ONE

Undeserved Grace

Scripture focus: Mark 7:24-37

Jesus got up and went away from there to the region of Tyre. And when He had entered a house, He wanted no one to know of it; yet He could not escape notice. But after hearing of Him, a woman whose little daughter had an unclean spirit immediately came and fell at His feet. Now the woman was a Gentile, of the Syrophoenician race. And she kept asking Him to cast the demon out of her daughter. And He was saying to her, "Let the children be satisfied first, for it is not good to take the children's bread and throw it to the dogs." But she answered and said to Him, "Yes, Lord, but even the dogs under the table feed on the children's crumbs." And He said to her, "Because of this answer go; the demon has gone out of your daughter." And going back to her home, she found the child lying on the bed, the demon having left.

Again He went out from the region of Tyre, and came through Sidon to the Sea of Galilee, within the region of Decapolis. They brought to Him one who was deaf and spoke with difficulty, and they implored Him to lay His hand on him. Jesus took him aside from the crowd, by himself, and put His fingers into his ears, and after spitting, He touched his tongue with the saliva; and looking up to heaven with a deep sigh, He said to him, "Ephphatha!" that is, "Be opened!" And his ears were opened, and the impediment of his tongue was removed, and he began speaking plainly. And He gave them orders not to tell anyone; but the more He ordered them, the more widely they continued to proclaim it. They were utterly astonished, saying, "He has done all things well; He makes even the deaf to hear and the mute to speak" (NASB).

Years ago my dad told me the story of a local policeman from our hometown who was known to have a very compassionate heart. Dad said one day the policeman was called to where a man was lying unconscious by a small farm road. Upon his arrival he realized the man was simply drunk. The policeman woke the man and began trying to get him to his car. The policeman was taken aback by the man's stench and demeanor and said to the drunk man, "I really shouldn't put someone like you into my clean car."

The drunk man quickly responded, "Well, I don't remember asking for a ride."

That story strikes me as both funny and heartbreaking. Hopefully the funny part is obvious. But I also hope the heartbreaking part is also obvious. This man had a soul that was being destroyed by his own bondage to reckless behavior.

Question: Does everyone, even people like this drunk man, deserve the grace of God?

This question comes to my mind as Jesus continues leading His apprentices on their three-year tour. The reason for my question is simple. Jesus' ministry seems, in this moment, to take a strange twist in Mark's writing. Jesus has given grace in so many circumstances. He has extended grace to crowds (6:30-31). He has extended grace to individuals (5:1-43). In His hometown (6:1-5) Jesus has extended grace. Even with

His enemies Jesus has extended grace (7:1-23). But now with a Gentile woman it seems that His grace has run out.

What has happened? Is Jesus just tired and in the flesh? Has Jesus had His fill of the brokenness of humanity? Could it be that He has grown weary of helping ungrateful people? Or could it be something else?

The answer is something else!

Jesus is teaching us about the beauty of underserved grace. Take time this week to search the Scriptures deeply to discover this beauty for yourself.

Allow me to help you to get a good start by focusing on the theological significance of what Jesus said and then the practical application:

- Theological significance:
  o Salvation finds its beginning point with one of the Jewish people. His name is Jesus (Acts 3:26; 4:12).

  o Salvation is not given to those who reject Jesus (Matthew 7:6).

  o Salvation is never earned or deserved (Matthew 11:20-24).

  o Salvation is for all who believe on Jesus (Romans 10:9-13).

- Practical application:
  o Those who receive this underserved grace recognize the theological truths listed above.

  o Such people know of their inability to save themselves.

- Such people repent of their sinful lifestyle.
- Such people believe God offers them what they do not deserve.

The Gentile woman evidenced both the theological and practical understanding of what Jesus said. One thing stood out to her. Despite her undeserved status, she knew Jesus would give her, if she asked, undeserved grace. This is true faith.

After this moment Mark again shows us the blessing of undeserved grace as Jesus is shown healing the blind man.

It is my prayer that God will refresh you as you study undeserved grace this week. It is also my prayer that God will place you in circumstances where you will share God's undeserved grace with others.

Here are our assignments for the week:

DAY 1:
Read Acts 3 and answer the following questions.
- Why did God offer grace to Israel before the rest of the world? Explain.
- What would have happened if Israel had embraced Jesus as the Messiah?

DAY 2:
Read John 4 and answer the following questions.
- Why did the woman at the well come to draw water in the heat of the day?
- What truth did this woman hear for the first time? Explain.

DAY 3:
Read Matthew 7 and answer the following questions.

- What did it mean when Jesus said, "Do not cast your pearls before swine"?
- What are the reasons people would die without receiving the grace of God? Explain.

DAY 4:

Read Romans 2 and answer the following questions.

- Why did the Jewish people see themselves as different from the rest of sinful humanity?
- What advantage did the Jewish people have over the rest of humanity? Explain.

DAY 5:

Read Romans 3 and answer the following questions.

- Is everyone born as a sinner under the wrath of God? Defend your answer.
- Why did God the Father accept Jesus' sacrifice for our sins?

WEEK TWENTY-TWO

Let's Try This Again

Scripture focus: Mark 8:1-21

In those days, when there was again a large crowd and they had nothing to eat, Jesus called His disciples and said to them, "I feel compassion for the people because they have remained with Me now three days and have nothing to eat. If I send them away hungry to their homes, they will faint on the way; and some of them have come from a great distance." And His disciples answered Him, "Where will anyone be able to find enough bread here in this desolate place to satisfy these people?" And He was asking them, "How many loaves do you have?" And they said, "Seven." And He directed the people to sit down on the ground; and taking the seven loaves, He gave thanks and broke them, and started giving them to His disciples to serve to them, and they served them to the people. They also had a few small fish; and after He had blessed them, He ordered these to be served as well. And they ate and were satisfied; and they picked up seven large baskets full of what was left over of the broken pieces. About four thousand were there; and He sent them away. And immediately He entered the boat with His disciples and came to the district of Dalmanutha.

The Pharisees came out and began to argue with Him, seeking from Him a sign from heaven, to test Him. Sighing deeply in His spirit, He said, "Why does this generation seek for a sign? Truly I say to you, no sign will be given to this generation." Leaving them, He again embarked and went away to the other side.

And they had forgotten to take bread, and did not have more than one loaf in the boat with them. And He was giving orders to them, saying, "Watch out! Beware of the leaven of the Pharisees and the leaven of Herod." They began to discuss with one another the fact that they had no bread. And Jesus, aware of this, said to them, "Why do you discuss the fact that you have no bread? Do you not yet see or understand? Do you have a hardened heart? HAVING EYES, DO YOU NOT SEE? AND HAVING EARS, DO YOU NOT HEAR? AND DO YOU NOT REMEMBER, when I broke the five loaves for the five thousand, how many baskets full of broken pieces you picked up?" They said to Him, "Twelve." "When I broke the seven for the four thousand, how many large baskets full of broken pieces did you pick up?" And they said to Him, "Seven." And He was saying to them, "Do you not yet understand?" (NASB).

It is said that it takes thirty days to either develop a habit or to break a habit. Question: Is this true in your life? Here is an honest admission: I have often had to learn things repeatedly.

This week we come to a familiar place with Jesus. It is a place we have been before. But this time the truth of what we will see is even deeper. Here is an amazing fact: God wastes nothing. Even though we sometimes get extremely frustrated with ourselves for not staying focused on what we know, our God still has great purpose for us.

Consider the first apprentices of Jesus. They had been following Jesus for far longer than thirty days. One would think they would have developed habits of faith that were exemplary for us. The truth is, it would be only after the resurrection of Jesus when the Holy Spirit

was given that these men would come into their own in living lives of example.

The words of Paul come rushing into my mind. Notice the weight of them:

You then, my child, be strengthened by the grace that is in Christ Jesus, and what you have heard from me in the presence of many witnesses entrust to faithful men, who will be able to teach others also (2 Timothy 2:1-2).

Brothers and sisters, it takes time to develop habits of great faith. Often we must be reminded of faith habits simply because it is easy to become familiar with the routine of faith. This routine leads to a slow fade of faith. Just because we have done something many times does not mean we have mastered it.

God often must place us in a moment of trial so we can both mentally and spiritually be brought back to what He was trying to instill in us. At other times God places a test before us as is the case in Mark 8. These tests are so we can know how we have matured in Christ.

What test are you facing this day? In our readings this week we will be brought face to face with what God wants us to be and how we get there. Please do not disregard the test or deny the test. Allow God to use the test so that you can get it in the faith journey you are on.

For a moment let's look at the test before the apprentices. Again, this is a familiar place. Jesus has been ministering to a large crowd of people (four thousand men plus women and children). At the end of day three Jesus says to the apprentices, "I have compassion on the crowd because they have been with me now three days and have nothing to eat. And I am unwilling to send them away hungry, lest they faint on the way" (Matthew 15:32).

In laymen's terms Jesus is asking, "What should we be doing for those who need our help?" This is oh-so-familiar ground. Two chapters earlier Jesus fed the five thousand and then walked on the water to the apprentices amid their storm. He had healed the sick and removed demons from a demon-possessed man.

The apprentices were ready for this, right? Wrong. They blew it. They went back to their old way of thinking. This is an impossible assignment.

Once again we see our loving Savior teaching the apprentices about who He is. Jesus is the God of compassion who has all power. Jesus is the God of compassion who wants us to walk in His power. Jesus is the God of clarity who wants us to overcome the carnal view of the world, which fills itself with wanting signs and easy faith.

Each time God places a test before you He is simply teaching you more and more of who He is and more and more about what He can do in your life. Take time this week to see the Lord as He is, and take time to see where you are with the Lord. Spend time seeking His assignments for your journey of faith. Spend time allowing God to stretch you in faith.

I can imagine the people considering the hands of Jesus as he continues to break off the bread from the loaves. When will it run out? Answer: only when everyone has enough. Wow--we serve a great God!

Here are our assignments for the week:

DAY 1:
Read Matthew 16 and answer the following questions.
- Who is the one who provides for the church? Why do we struggle with trusting in our provider?
- Why is the truth of the Cross so hard for the world to accept? Explain.

DAY 2:
Read Hebrews 10 and answer the following questions.

- What is the benefit of endurance?
- Why do trials sometimes lead to the weakening of faith? Explain.

DAY 3:

Read Psalm 9 and answer the following questions.
- What does the sovereignty of God mean to you personally?
- Does God really have the final say in the events of people's lives? Explain.

DAY 4:

Read Psalm 119 and answer the following questions.
- How does the Word of God keep you from sin?
- How does the Word of God help you to defeat false teaching?

DAY 5:

Read 1 Kings 18 and answer the following questions.
- Why was Elijah being challenged by Ahab?
- What issues in our day demand an Elijah-like faith? Explain.

WEEK TWENTY-THREE

What Do You See?

Scripture focus: Mark 8:22-26

*A*nd *they came to Bethsaida. And they brought a blind man to Jesus and implored Him to touch him. Taking the blind man by the hand, He brought him out of the village; and after spitting on his eyes and laying His hands on him, He asked him, "Do you see anything?" And he looked up and said, "I see men, for I see them like trees, walking around." Then again He laid His hands on his eyes; and he looked intently and was restored, and began to see everything clearly. And He sent him to his home, saying, "Do not even enter the village" (NASB).*

In the ABC sitcom The Middle there's an episode where the father, Mike Heck, invites his youngest son, Brick who is a bookworm, to go fishing with him. Brick goes to the library and checks out all kinds of books on fishing. The scene shifts to the lake where they're fishing. There Dad is fishing with Brick, who is sitting reading a book about fishing. Finally Mike comments, "Brick, you'll enjoy this only if you're trying it instead of just reading about it."

How often do we find ourselves missing out on the Christian life because we're doing something else instead of experiencing life with Jesus? Is it just a sight (perspective) problem?

There are times when I'm preoccupied with other things as I do life. I'm texting when I should be watching. I'm reading when I should be experiencing. I'm too busy to understand what's most important. I'm frightened about what it would take to live the Christian life. And sometimes honestly I just don't care.

This week you will be challenged in your readings to understand that your eyes are only the lens to your heart and mind. It is the condition of your mind and heart that determines your reactions and your actions in the Christian life.

Before we begin our weekday assignments, let's look at our Scripture focus for the week. The Bible says Jesus came to Bethsaida. This city was located on the northern shore of the Sea of Galilee. Jesus did many miracles in this place (Matthew 11:21). Dr. Halley observes, "This is near where Jesus fed the 5000 men" (Halley's Bible Handbook, 635).

It was home to Peter, Andrew, and Phillip (John 1:34-50). There is a lot of history in this place. We see an example in Luke 5. Without doubt there was a lot of hurt in this city. Being a fishing town, there had to be examples of fisherman who drowned in storms or in boating accidents. There had to be stories of lonely nights with no catch and long days of mending nets and repairing boats.

We know one family hurt because one of the members was blind. We know this man was loved because his friends brought him to Jesus.

Here is a statement about every city in the world: "The city is filled with people who are headed either to heaven or hell." Allow that to sink in before I ask you this question. Now here is the question: What do you see in your city?

In this short section of Mark 8 God wants us to see four things about our Lord and Savior, Jesus. Please take time to clear your mind and heart so you can see them.

We see Jesus as a personal God. Jesus comes to this city and allows individuals to approach Him. He then takes an individual away from the crowd so there is undivided attention. This is the heart of John 3:16.

We see Jesus as a merciful God. Jesus is willing to help this man. The Bible says Jesus spit in his eyes. Now there is much debate here as to why. I believe Spurgeon's ageless commentary is closest to what we need to see about this:

"Had our Lord cast all his miracles in one mold, men would have attached undue importance to the manner by which He did the miracle and they would have bypassed looking at the mercy of the one who did the miracle. God made a connection with this man so to test this man to see if he would have faith to believe" (Charles H. Spurgeon, [NEED TITLE], 25).

We see Jesus as a revealing God. When this man opens his eyes, he sees a little and will now be willing to see even more. What a picture of our spiritual development! When we first come to Christ we are new creations (2 Corinthians 5:17), but we are also babes in Christ (2 Peter 3:1-2) who need to develop strong spiritual eyes (Colossians 1:9-10). This is a process of growth, and we seek the daily revealing of God.

We see Jesus as one who is worthy of praise. Jesus did not want the man to go into the city to tell everyone of the miracle, because He already had multitudes who were following Him for miracles only. I suspect this man had to tell others what Jesus had done for him.

Take the time this week as you read each passage to allow God to reveal more and more of himself to you. Pay close attention to what could move your eyes in different directions. Submit to God's look and seek God's heart. It's going to be a great week.

Here are our assignments for the week:

DAY 1:
Read John 5 and answer the following questions.
- Take time to research the place where Jesus met this crippled man. Write down your findings.
- Take time to research the place where you currently live. Write down your findings.

Day 2:
Read Luke 10 and answer the following questions.
- Why did the religious leaders decide not to help their fellow man?
- Why do we sometimes decide not to help our fellow man?

Day 3:
Read Joshua 6 and answer the following questions.
- What did the people see as they walked around the outer walls of the city of Jericho?
- What type of faith does it require to believe in what you do not see? Explain.

Day 4:
Read Isaiah 6 and answer the following questions.
- Describe what Isaiah saw when he was in the house of the Lord.
- What effect did this encounter with God have on Isaiah's life?

Day 5:
Read Psalm 11 and answer the following questions.
- What does the Lord see each day?
- What does the Lord see in your life each day?

The Floor is Yours

Scripture focus: Mark 8:27-30

*J*esus went out, along with His disciples, to the villages of Caesarea Philippi; and on the way He questioned His disciples, saying to them, "Who do people say that I am?" They told Him, saying, "John the Baptist; and others say Elijah; but others, one of the prophets." And He continued by questioning them, "But who do you say that I am?" Peter answered and said to Him, "You are the Christ." And He warned them to tell no one about Him (*NASB*).

I magine being asked to represent Jesus in a debate setting at a secular college. You accept the invitation because you know you are to always be ready to give a defense for the faith that is yours (1 Peter 3:15). But as the debate gets closer and closer you find yourself wondering, Do I know enough to clearly state the truth of who Jesus is?

You study for an entire month. You have all the resources you can find. Your church is praying, and every person you know who will pray you have asked to pray. Now it is time. The opposite side is to present their case. As you listen it is clear they have no argument for why Jesus is purportedly not real. Finally after what seems an eternity, the defense is over. Now the moderator looks to you and says, "The floor is yours."

Question: Are you ready?

This week our Scripture focus finds us on the heels of Jesus' miracle of healing the blind man. Now Jesus begins to turn His ministry toward teaching the apprentices about His coming crucifixion, death, and resurrection. By this point the apprentices have been in the classroom of teaching for over two years. They have experienced miracle after miracle. Now the teaching would become more intense.

But before the lessons begin, Jesus turns to the disciples with two questions:

1. Who do men say that I am?
2. Who do you say that I am?

It is as if Jesus says, "The floor is yours."

The first question was easy. All they had to do was to simply state what they had heard. But the second question was not as easy. The apprentices were being asked to share what they had come to a settled view about.

This week you will be challenged by the reading assignments. The challenge will be to read what the Bible says and then form your views. The truth is, often our views are solely formed by what others have taught us. We have to be careful when we just assume our teacher is correct. What if his or her views are biased, prejudiced, or misinformed?

You and I get in a mess when we equate people's views with those of God's Word. This's why I preach God's Word. His Word is the same no matter how I feel or how I've acted in the day. First Baptist Church of Jackson is committed to teaching God's Word.

This week I want to challenge you to form your views based upon God's Word. Peter was able to give the right answer to question number two because he believed God's Word on the subject. It was God himself who revealed to Peter the truth about the Christ.

God does not have to reveal himself to us, but He does so in love. I pray that you take time to investigate that love this week as you discover for yourself who Jesus is. As you study, if you realize that you don't know Jesus, please don't hide the truth. Embrace the truth and become a genuine Christ-follower.

Because of what Peter discovered, the floor he spoke from was secure in Acts 2. Because of what Peter discovered, the floor of his future was significant because his life was founded on the Rock of ages (1 Peter 1:3-4).

Here are our assignments for the week:

DAY 1:

Read 1 Peter 2 and answer the following questions.
- Why is Christ described as the "Living Stone" and why are Christians described as "living stones"?
- Why do some people struggle to accept the Living Stone, and what happens if they do not accept Him?

DAY 2:

Read Isaiah 43 and answer the following question.
- Who is this one described as Israel's Savior? Explain your answer.
- Describe the work of this Savior as recorded in Isaiah 43.

DAY 3:

Read Psalm 118 and answer the following questions.
- Why is it harder to trust in God rather than people?
- Write down some of the things you're trusting God for.

DAY 4:

Read Matthew 16:16-23 and answer the following questions.

- Define the title "Christ."
- Who is the Rock? Defend your answer.

DAY 5:

Read Galatians 1 and answer the following questions.

- How was Paul able to understand who Jesus really is?
- How important is it to correctly understand who Jesus is?

Changing One's Mind

Scripture focus: Mark 8:31--9:1

*A*nd He began to teach them that the Son of Man must suffer *many things and be rejected by the elders and the chief priests and the scribes, and be killed, and after three days rise again. And He was stating the matter plainly. And Peter took Him aside and began to rebuke Him. But turning around and seeing His disciples, He rebuked Peter and said, "Get behind Me, Satan; for you are not setting your mind on God's interests, but man's."*

And He summoned the crowd with His disciples, and said to them, "If anyone wishes to come after Me, he must deny himself, and take up his cross and follow Me. For whoever wishes to save his life will lose it, but whoever loses his life for My sake and the gospel's will save it. For what does it profit a man to gain the whole world, and forfeit his soul? For what will a man give in exchange for his soul? For whoever is ashamed of Me and My words in this adulterous and sinful generation, the Son of Man will also be ashamed of him when He comes in the glory of His Father with the holy angels."

And Jesus was saying to them, "Truly I say to you, there are some of those who are standing here who will not taste death until they see the kingdom of God after it has come with power" (NASB).

A famous line in the discussion of the differences between men and women is simply "It's a woman's prerogative to change her mind." And all the men who read this heartily cry out, "Amen!"

Question: Have you ever had something on your mind that you could not get off your mind? My precious wife sometimes will wake up in the night and can't go back to sleep because her mind cannot disengage. At other times I find myself missing out on important instructions because I have my mind set in a particular direction.

This week we will focus our attention to this subject of the mind. In writing to the church at Philippi, Paul made it clear in Philippians 2:5--"Let this mind be in you, which was also in Christ Jesus" (KJV). Paul goes on in that chapter to describe the outworkings of Jesus' mind-set.

As we come to our Scripture focus for the week, it is clear as to what Jesus' mind-set is. The apprentices were asked a question and given the floor to answer it. They answered correctly (8:27-30). In their minds they understood both who Jesus was and what He needed to do.

Now don't just slip right on by the last sentence. In the apprentices' minds they understood both who Jesus was and what Jesus needed to do. But it was not correct. Peter's mind was set as to what Jesus' next move should be. He was a popular man who certainly had the power of God on his life. He was God's Son. In Peter's mind, all that was left was for Jesus to form an army, maybe an angel army, and take over.

But Jesus would speak in a way that would seek to change Peter's mind. As you read about this strong encounter you will be challenged to consider the importance of the Cross and the importance of genuine discipleship.

Jesus' first attempt to change Peter's mind was in His teaching about what the mission was about. He said He would suffer, be rejected, killed, and raised from the dead on the third day. Mark helps us to understand that Jesus' teaching here was not in a parable but was in clear and simple language, so much so that Peter got upset. The ESV translates his response as "took him aside and began to rebuke him" (Mark 8:32). The word "rebuke" is a word that we're not very familiar with. The New Living Translation puts it in language of our day: "Peter took him aside and began to reprimand him for saying such things." In Matthew's account we find what Peter said: "Far be it from you, Lord! This shall never happen to you" (Matthew 16:22).

In turn Jesus rebukes Peter. Christ opens our eyes to where Peter's mind was focused. Literally Peter's mind was dwelling on the wrong path. Think through this for a moment. Have you and I ever had our minds on the wrong path? Jesus helps us to see the wrong path for what it is:

- Peter's mind was in a worldly path.
- Peter's mind was filled with emotion.
- Peter's mind was being used by Satan.
- Peter's mind was a stumbling block to the gospel.

Think this through: if Jesus had given in to Peter's mind-set, the only hope of our world would have been lost. The direction of our mind has great impact on lives. So let me ask you: "Where is your mind as you read this week's devotion?" Do you need a mind change?

Jesus teaches us how to have that mind change in verse 34. Look up the word "deny," and take time to discover what it means to carry a cross. Enjoy this week as God changes your mind.

Here are our assignments for the week:

DAY 1:

Read Isaiah 55 and answer the following questions.

- In our world of competing voices for our mind, what does Isaiah mean by "incline your ear"?
- Why are God's thoughts different from our thoughts, and what are God's thoughts about where you are in life?

DAY 2:

Read Romans 13 and answer the following questions.

- In our world of unrest and political resistance, we find people who will not obey government in any way. What is God's mind on this subject?
- The widespread thought of our day is this: "You really don't have to be that different to live the Christian life." What is God's mind on this subject?

DAY 3:

Read Psalm 49 and answer the following questions.

- Do the riches of this world affect how we view life?
- What does God have to say about our ability to help each other?

DAY 4:

Read 2 Peter 1 and answer the following questions.

- Why did Peter have confidence even though he was within a year of death?
- What would Peter teach us to put into our minds today?

DAY 5:

Read Philippians 2 and answer the following questions.

- Why was the church struggling with having the mind of Christ?
- When we have the mind of Christ we will have a servant heart. What does this look like in our day?

A Moment of Unveiling

Scripture focus: Mark 9:2-13

*S*ix *days later, Jesus took with Him Peter and* [a]*James and John, and brought them up on a high mountain by themselves. And He was transfigured before them; and His garments became radiant and exceedingly white, as no launderer on earth can whiten them. Elijah appeared to them along with Moses; and they were talking with Jesus. Peter said to Jesus, "Rabbi, it is good for us to be here; let us make three tabernacles, one for You, and one for Moses, and one for Elijah." For he did not know what to answer; for they became terrified. Then a cloud formed, overshadowing them, and a voice came out of the cloud, "This is My beloved Son, listen to Him!" All at once they looked around and saw no one with them anymore, except Jesus alone.*

As they were coming down from the mountain, He gave them orders not to relate to anyone what they had seen, until the Son of Man rose from the dead. They seized upon that statement, discussing with one another what rising from the dead meant. They asked Him, saying, "Why is it that the scribes say that Elijah must come first?" And He said to them, "Elijah does first come and restore all things. And yet how is it written of the Son of

Man that He will suffer many things and be treated with contempt? But I say to you that Elijah has indeed come, and they did to him whatever they wished, just as it is written of him" (NASB).

There are moments when I just can't seem to get my point across. I do my best to explain my point, and I even go to the effort of illustrating it. Still yet, my point remains a mystery to those who have heard me share it. You ask, "What are you talking about?" You see, you just proved my point. The point is, God has truth for us that is sometimes veiled in our inability either to share the truth or to grasp the truth.

This week's Scripture focus seeks to reveal the truth of the importance of the cross of Jesus. But to those who were struggling with this truth, even a moment of unveiling was not enough. Who were these people? These were Jesus' apprentices. These were the twelve who were closest to the Lord Jesus in His earthly ministry. These were the guys who, if anyone got it, it should have been them. But the unveiling left them even more confused.

Take time to read all three parallel accounts of this unveiling: Matthew 17:1-8; Luke 9:28-36; and our Scripture focus for the week.

The moment in time is clear. Six days earlier, Jesus had informed the apprentices of the coming of the Cross and the glorious Resurrection. The disciples did not want to see Jesus going through suffering. The disciples were hopeful Jesus would establish the kingdom apart from a cross.

This moment in time becomes complex. As these men were struggling to get the point, Jesus took the inner circle (Peter, John, and James) to the top of a mountain to join Him in prayer (Luke 9:28). As He prayed, suddenly His appearance was altered (transformed). Matthew writes, "His face shone like the sun" (17:2). Mark writes, "his garments became glistering, exceeding white, so as no fuller on earth can whiten them" (9:3). In this moment Jesus' glory, which had been veiled in humanity, came through. The apprentices g0t a glimpse of what Jesus would look like for all eternity.

Suddenly two men in white apparel were standing by Jesus. Before we have time to speculate as to who they were, Mark tells us it was Moses and Elijah. Moses was the great law-giver to Israel, and Elijah was the greatest prophet who protected and stood for the Law of God. We wonder, What were they talking about? But we do not have to wonder. Luke unveils the answer. They were talking about His departure (Luke 9:31).

Peter is in shock overload. He tries to talk his way through this moment of unveiling. He thinks out loud. He wants to build three monuments to celebrate what he believes is the kingdom that has come. He did not realize what He was saying.

The moment becomes even more complex when the glory cloud of God descends on the mountain with God's voice speaking clearly, "This is My beloved Son, listen to Him!" (NASB)--literally "Be obedient to Him!"

In this moment we must ask, Did these guys understand the point of what Jesus was saying? Our answer comes in the conversation the apprentices had with Jesus coming down the mountain. These guys totally believed Jesus was the Messiah. They knew He was fulfilling all the teachings of the Law and the Prophets. But they could not understand the Cross. They turned their attention to prophecies of Malachi. They wanted to know when Elijah would come and prepare the way.

We know that John the Baptist fulfilled the role of preparing the way for the first coming, and we believe Elijah could be one of the witnesses in Revelation 11 preparing people for the Second Coming. However, these apprentices still struggled to understand the unveiling of the Cross. It would only be after His resurrection that they would get the point.

This week you will interact with Scripture that will stretch and illuminate your understanding of the power of the Cross. There are many things about our faith that will not be unveiled until it has accomplished its work in your life. Before you read each day's assignment, make sure the power of the Cross is at work in your life.

Here are our assignments for the week:

DAY 1:
Read Romans 12 and answer the following questions.
- Paul encourages us to be "transformed in the renewing of our mind." What does this word *transformed* have in common with what happened with Jesus in Mark 9?
- What are the character traits we see in someone who has been transformed?

DAY 2:
Read Deuteronomy 18 and answer the following questions.
- What did Moses believe was the true hope of his people?
- How does God the Father's statement "Listen to Him!" apply to what we read in Deuteronomy 18?

DAY 3:
Read Exodus 40 and answer the following questions.
- How does the power of the Cross figure into our daily moments in life?
- What would happen if the people of God moved before the Lord's presence moved?

DAY 4:

Read Colossians 1 and answer the following questions.
- What light does the Cross bring into our lives?
- What areas of darkness does the Cross need to be applied to in your life?

DAY 5:

Read Colossians 2 and answer the following questions.
- How can the power of the Cross build your faith?
- Are there any sins that are more powerful than the Cross?

Meanwhile Back in the Trenches

Scripture focus: Mark 9:14-29

When they came back to the disciples, they saw a large crowd around them, and some scribes arguing with them. Immediately, when the entire crowd saw Him, they were amazed and began running up to greet Him. And He asked them, "What are you discussing with them?" And one of the crowd answered Him, "Teacher, I brought You my son, possessed with a spirit which makes him mute; and whenever it seizes him, it slams him to the ground and he foams at the mouth, and grinds his teeth and stiffens out. I told Your disciples to cast it out, and they could not do it." And He answered them and said, "O unbelieving generation, how long shall I be with you? How long shall I put up with you? Bring him to Me!" They brought the boy to Him. When he saw Him, immediately the spirit threw him into a convulsion, and falling to the ground, he began rolling around and foaming at the mouth. And He asked his father, "How long has this been happening to him?" And he said, "From childhood. It has often thrown him both into the fire and into the water to destroy him. But if You can do anything, take pity on us and help us!" And Jesus said to him, "'If You can?' All things are possible to him who believes." Immediately the boy's father cried out and said, "I do believe; help my unbelief." When Jesus saw that a crowd was rapidly gathering, He rebuked the unclean spirit, saying to it, "You deaf and mute spirit, I command you, come out of him and do not enter him again." After crying out and throwing him into terrible convulsions, it came out; and the boy became so much like a corpse that most of them said, "He is dead!" But Jesus took him by the hand and raised him; and he got up. When He came into the house, His disciples began questioning Him privately, "Why could we not drive it out?" And He said to them, "This kind cannot come out by anything but prayer" (NASB).

It was so awesome. The music was over the top. The preaching of the Word was with power, and the invitation was so clear. The people left the service with a confidence that could move mountains. But outside the service a large mountain loomed dark and treacherous.

You ask, "What Sunday are you referring to, and what large mountain loomed dark and treacherous?"

I'm referring to a typical Sunday at First Baptist Church of Jackson, and I'm also referring to the moment when Jesus came down from the Mount of Transfiguration with the inner group of disciples (Mark 9:9-13). Waiting either at the bottom of the mountain or just a little ways up was a scene that loomed large. Take time now to read Mark's account. Next read Matthew 17:14-19, and finally read Luke 9:37-42.

The other nine apprentices were down in the trenches waiting for the group to return. As they waited they noticed a large crowd coming toward them. In the crowd were scribes, and there was one man who came holding onto a teenage son. Something was obviously wrong with the son. The father spoke and told about the dark and treacherous problem that plagued their family.

I can hear one of the apprentice's responses: "No problem--bring him to us. We have experience with this sort of thing" (see Mark 6:7,

13). The apprentices place their hands on the teenager, but nothing happens. This is the enemy's opportunity to turn a faith moment into a chaotic moment. Here in the trenches faith is now in question.

But to the rescue of faith comes our Lord and Savior Jesus Christ. He calms the crowd with a question: "What are you arguing about with them?" The trench-warfare is laid out before Jesus. In this moment I want you to slow down with me and pay close attention to what Jesus says to the apprentices.

"O faithless generation, how long am I to be with you?"

Brothers and sisters, think about how much we benefit from the apprentices' successes and failures. We gain so much here. When you look at the parallel passages, you realize this is a faithful building moment in the trenches of life.

Hurt is the common experience of all people. However, hope is the uncommon experience of those who have faith.

We see this teenager being healed by Jesus. We see his father evidence small faith with an honest faith of needed help with unbelief. Jesus' words to the father stand as encouragement to all of us in the trenches. "All things are possible to those who believe in what God says."

Once the healing had been completed, the apprentices in private wanted to know why they failed in the trenches. Here is what Jesus taught them. Jesus turned to the mountain He had just descended from. I see Him pointing at the mountain as He says, "If you had the faith of a mustard seed, you could say to this mountain be moved and it would be moved into the sea."

The trenches of life are truly great mountains that are humanly impossible to move. Jesus proved His power in removing the mountain of demon possession from the young man. The apprentices had tried to move the mountain without prayer and without God's power.

Into our trenches we are to invite God to invade with His all-powerful hand to remove the enemy and to fill us with redeeming power. I want to challenge you to this kind of prayer this week. I want to challenge you to fast so that you can hear from God. As you read this week, it could be a faith-building week! So get to work moving that mountain.

Here are our assignments for the week:

DAY 1:

Read 1 John 5 and answer the following questions.
- What must be the first step in overcoming the world?
- What things do you need to overcome in this week?

DAY 2:

Read Exodus 14 and answer the following questions.
- How and why did the Israelites fail to have faith at the Red Sea?
- What faith-building moments are we facing in our nation? How can you make a difference?

DAY 3:

Read Acts 5 and answer the following questions.
- How does the personal desire for approval affect trench warfare?
- What could happen if we were able to overcome the mountain of fear in our faith?

DAY 4:

Read Acts 16 and answer the following questions.
- What role does prayer play in trench warfare?
- Why did the jailor believe in what his prisoners had to say?

DAY 5:

Read the book of Philemon and answer the following questions.

- What is the main point of this book?
- List the things you must forgive so that mountain faith can happen.

It's Coming Out

Scripture focus: Mark 9:30-41

*A*nd they went forth from thence, and passed through Galilee; and he would not that any man should know it. For he taught his disciples, and said unto them, The Son of man is delivered up into the hands of men, and they shall kill him; and when he is killed, after three days he shall rise again. But they understood not the saying, and were afraid to ask him.*

And they came to Capernaum: and when he was in the house he asked them, What were ye reasoning on the way? But they held their peace: for they had disputed one with another on the way, who was the greatest. And he sat down, and called the twelve; and he saith unto them, If any man would be first, he shall be last of all, and servant of all. And he took a little child, and set him in the midst of them: and taking him in his arms, he said unto them, Whosoever shall receive one of such little children in my name, receiveth me: and whosoever receiveth me, receiveth not me, but him that sent me. John said unto him, Teacher, we saw one casting out demons in thy name; and we forbade him, because he followed not us. But Jesus said, Forbid him not: for there is no man who shall do a mighty work in my name, and be able quickly to speak evil of me. For he that is not against us is for us. For whosoever shall give you a cup of water to drink, because ye are Christ's, verily I say unto you, he shall in no wise lose his reward (NASB).

Matters of the heart often have a strange way of working themselves out into the open. For example, on the television sitcom M.A.S.H. there was a character by the name of Margaret Houlihan, the head of nursing in this M.A.S.H. unit in Korea. In one episode she finds a little dog and begins feeding it. A few days later the dog is killed. Margaret becomes extremely emotional as she gets the news. Here is a strong lady who was living with death and devastation every day. But on this day what was in her heart was coming out. She could no longer hold in what was breaking her heart day after day.

Write it down: Our Lord uses many different methods to reveal to us what is in our hearts. In our year-long journey with Jesus we have already experienced some of those methods. This week's scripture shows us another method. Jesus' chosen method is a question. The question seems to indicate that Jesus does not know what the guys had been arguing about. However, Luke in his account (9:47) reveals why Jesus asks the question: "Jesus saw the reasoning of their heart." As always Jesus knew what was in the apprentices' hearts. In the same way, Jesus knows what's in our hearts as well. Nothing is hidden from Him. His questions are for our revelation, not His.

The apprentices could not get things straight in their minds or in their hearts concerning the kingdom of God. They still believed Jesus was going to establish an earthly kingdom. They were arguing as to who would be highest in authority in Jesus' kingdom.

The answer to that question unearths two very essential questions: How does one become a citizen of God's kingdom? What is true greatness before God?

I realize the wide diversity of responses to the questions above. I know some of our sheep will have a false humility that says, "I just hope I get into heaven." Still others have what I call a freeloading humility. Such people say humble things like "I could never do good things." The truth is that such a person is using this freeloading humility to excuse his or her laziness of faith.

Jesus answers both the above questions in His teaching application. He calls for a young child to come to Him. The child comes in obedience and trusts Jesus to care for him. This is the illustration of how one becomes a citizen of God's kingdom. He or she must have a childlike obedience and faith in Jesus alone. This is the heart of Paul's teaching in Romans 10:9-10.

As Jesus continues to hold this child (I believe on His lap), He unloads the truest indicator of greatness in God's eyes. Allow your eyes to slowly process the following: "If anyone would be first, he must be last of all and servant of all." The truth of this statement is given over and over in Scripture.

This week I want to challenge you to spend time examining the life of service. Literally the word service is translated in the Greek as slave. Over and over the apostles speak of their lives as being those of a "slave of Jesus Christ."

Here is an important warning: "The subject matter of Jesus is highly offensive to many in the church world today." You may even be offended yourself. Pay attention to how Jesus speaks about the treatment of a child. Pay attention to how Jesus spends extended time warning us against those things that would cause us to be offensive to the life of obedience and faith.

Finally, allow yourself to deal with the place where non-kingdom citizens will spend eternity. Yes, hell is real. All who find themselves offended by Jesus will receive the reward of their rebellion and rejection.

Please allow God to work in you to reveal what is in your heart.

Here are our assignments for the week:

DAY 1:

Read Hebrews 4 and answer the following questions.

- Why do we need God's Word to reveal what is in our hearts?
- What happens when we disregard what God reveals about our hearts?

DAY 2:

Read Ephesians 6: 5-9 and answer the following questions.

- Is the Bible suggesting the acceptance of slavery in any form or fashion? Explain.
- What can we gain from Paul's teaching concerning the attitude of one who serves others?

DAY 3:

Read 1 Corinthians 10 and answer the following questions.

- Why did Israel fail so miserably with the temptations placed before her?
- What does Paul mean by "the way of escape"?

DAY 4:

Read Matthew 23 and answer the following questions.

- How was it possible for the religious leaders to shut the kingdom of heaven in people's faces?
- What will hell be like?

DAY 5:

Read Galatians 4 and answer the following questions.

- The issue of slavery is mentioned often in this chapter. What is the difference between a slave and a son?
- What does Paul mean by being a slave of earthly principles?

WEEK TWENTY-NINE

Hell: Where Do You Stand?

Scripture focus: Mark 9:42-50

*W*hoever causes one of these little ones who believe to stumble, it would be better for him if, with a heavy millstone hung around his neck, he had been cast into the sea. If your hand causes you to stumble, cut it off; it is better for you to enter life crippled, than, having your two hands, to go into hell, into the unquenchable fire, [where THEIR WORM DOES NOT DIE, AND THE FIRE IS NOT QUENCHED.] If your foot causes you to stumble, cut it off; it is better for you to enter life lame, than, having your two feet, to be cast into hell, [where THEIR WORM DOES NOT DIE, AND THE FIRE IS NOT QUENCHED.] If your eye causes you to stumble, throw it out; it is better for you to enter the kingdom of God with one eye, than, having two eyes, to be cast into hell, where THEIR WORM DOES NOT DIE, AND THE FIRE IS NOT QUENCHED.*

"*FOR EVERYONE WILL BE SALTED WITH FIRE. Salt is good; but if the salt becomes unsalty, with what will you make it salty again? Have salt in yourselves, and be at peace with one another*" (NASB).

As I sit at my home office writing this devotion, I'm writing with an extremely sad heart because of the news of tragedy filling my mind. A teenager in our local high school has lost her life after a tragic accident. About an hour ago I finished meeting with a group of guys who were trying to figure out who might have known this girl.

For me the struggle was personal because I feel, as did Paul in Romans 1, that I am under obligation to share the gospel with all people. It is my desire, as it is my Lord's desire, for all people to be saved. One of the Internet posts I read was as follows: "I really do not know where this teenager was with the Lord."

One might conclude the same about the apprentices at in Mark 9. Here were guys who were struggling with the truth of the Cross. In their minds they could not possibly see any reason that Jesus needed to go to the cross. In the verses before us this week we see three reasons:

- The coming judgment of God

- The reality of heaven

- The reality of hell

These form for us a reason to sing praises about "the wondrous cross." They form for us a burning theology of getting people to the Cross. The words of the refrain of an old hymn ring so true: At the cross, at the cross, where I first saw the light, / And the burden of my heart rolled away, / It was there by faith I received my sight, / And now I am happy all the day (Ralph Hudson, 1885).

This week I want to direct you to focus on one the reasons we need the Cross: the reality of hell. In context Halley writes, "A supreme Christian motive for living a godly life is so that no one else may be lost on account of our example" (Halley's Bible Handbook, 636).

This truth leads us to even do radical discipleship for the seriousness of the cause. Jesus is not suggesting that we pluck out our eyes, cut off our hands, or saw off our feet. Jesus is teaching us about how quickly and decisively we must live to place a light in front of others.

Brothers and sisters, the reality of hell leads me to radical discipleship. I know judgment is coming to all people. I know that those who have rejected Jesus, never heard of Jesus, or have chosen to ride the fence regarding Jesus will spend eternity in hell. Think through this. Hell is a place of unquenchable fire. This place has only an entrance and no exits. This place is where each person will spend eternity. The Bible speaks about an internal (one does not die) and external (flames) pain that leads to weeping and gnashing of teeth.

I have inserted the following commentary for clarity:

The Greek word geenna ("Gehenna," trans. "hell") is transliterated from two Hebrew words meaning "Valley of Hinnom," a place south of Jerusalem where children were once sacrificed to the pagan god Molech (2 Chron. 28:3; 33:6; Jer. 7:31; 19:5–6; 32:35). Later, during the reforms of Josiah (2 Kings 23:10) the site became Jerusalem's refuse dump where fires burned continually to consume regular deposits of worm-infested garbage. In Jewish thought the imagery of fire and worms vividly portrayed the place of future eternal punishment for the wicked (cf. the apocryphal Judith 16:17 and Ecclesiasticus 7:17). Jesus used the word geenna in 11 of its 12 New Testament occurrences (the one exception is James 3:6) (

John D. Grassmick, "Mark," in The Bible Knowledge Commentary: An Exposition of the Scriptures, ed. J. F. Walvoord and R. B. Zuck, vol. 2 [Wheaton, Ill.: Victor Books, 1985, 147]).

This is why Jesus was going to the Cross. Jesus knew of the reality of hell. Jesus loved us so much that He came so that we would not have to go to hell (John 3:16). This week's readings will challenge you to drink deeply concerning the subject of hell and will cause you to consider your role in the Kingdom.

Here are our assignments for the week:

DAY 1:

Read Matthew 18 and answer the following questions.

- Why would it be better to die than to cause someone to miss heaven?
- Why are lost people so valuable to Jesus?

DAY 2:

Read John 6 and answer the following questions.

- How does Jesus' bread from heaven keep a person out of hell?
- What is the opposite of living forever? Explain.

DAY 3:

Read Luke 12 and answer the following questions.

- Why is Jesus to be feared more than people?
- How does knowing Jesus change your approach to dealing with people?

DAY 4:

Read Matthew 13 and answer the following questions.

- What does Jesus mean by "the harvest at the end of the age?"
- Who are the reapers in this text?

DAY 5:

Read Revelation 14 and answer the following questions.

- What will happen to the nations of the world on judgment day?
- Where will you be on judgment day? Explain.

WEEK THIRTY

Marital Suicide

Scripture focus: Mark 10:1-12

*G*etting up, He went from there to the region of Judea and beyond the Jordan; crowds gathered around Him again, and, according to His custom, He once more began to teach them.

Some Pharisees came up to Jesus, testing Him, and began to question Him whether it was lawful for a man to divorce a wife. And He answered and said to them, "What did Moses command you?" They said, "Moses permitted a man TO WRITE A CERTIFICATE OF DIVORCE AND SEND *her* AWAY.*" But Jesus said to them, "Because of your hardness of heart he wrote you this commandment. But from the beginning of creation, God* MADE THEM MALE AND FEMALE. FOR THIS REASON A MAN SHALL LEAVE HIS FATHER AND MOTHER[D], AND THE TWO SHALL BECOME ONE FLESH; SO THEY ARE NO LONGER TWO, BUT ONE FLESH. *What therefore God has joined together, let no man separate."*

In the house the disciples began questioning Him about this again. And He said to them, "Whoever divorces his wife and marries another woman commits adultery against her; and if she herself divorces her husband and marries another man, she is committing adultery" (NASB).

One of the awesome things about reading through the Bible is the holistic approach to every area of our lives. When people just randomly select books to read or selected chapters to read, they are prone to study only their likes or what they're already successful with. We desperately need to study all of God's Word (see 2 Timothy 3:16).

This week's Scripture focus is a case in point. Before us is Jesus' teaching concerning the subject of marital suicide.

Keep in mind that wherever Jesus went the crowds were large and the blessings were unbelievable. One of those blessings happened when Jesus was challenged by the religious leaders. Often they would come with a topic that they hoped would stump Jesus. In doing so, they wanted to prove that He was not the Son of God.

Every time the religious crowd was around Jesus, it was Apologetics 101. We read questions of theology or questions of practicality. For His apprentices, and for us who follow Jesus, these encounters give us some of the most detailed answers to the toughest questions of life.

Case in point--our scriptural focus of the week: The religious leaders come with a question that still plagues our society to this day: What is God's view concerning divorce?

The religious leaders placed before Jesus the teaching of Moses. They argued, "Moses allowed it." This, by the way, is the common viewpoint of our society. Humanity begins life with a heart-view that says, "Nothing is forever." Humanity spurns a poison that oozes from a wicked heart. This poison is simply "All of life is about me." Every circle, every institution, every breath, and every god exists for me.

However, the viewpoint of God is radically different. In Jesus' response, we are taken back past Moses' day to the day when God instituted marriage in Genesis 2. Jesus quotes from this passage because He was there in Genesis 2. He is, according to Colossians 1:15, the creator of all things, including man.

Jesus gives us God's design for marriage: God intends for one man and one woman to live their lives together for a lifetime. He wants them to leave the singleness behind and embrace a new singleness (verse 7). God's design was for marriage to create on new life together (verse 8). God's design was for the couple to live together under the headship of Christ (verse 9).

But by Jesus' days on the earth the hardness of men's hearts had polluted their view and pointed marriage in a different direction. Here is a sampling of the direction: One man and one woman co-exist. Each brings his or her dysfunction into the marriage. Each holds back part of himself or herself for exclusive rights. There are two separate lives under one roof. Each person lives life on his or her own terms.

What Jesus was dealing with was simply "marital suicide."

As you move through the daily readings this week you will be challenged to walk through what God has to say concerning marriage. You will be asked to honestly and genuinely focus on your present views. One footnote: Be careful in this week, because your heart can fool you into believing that your present way is perfect. Take time to detox and allow the Holy Spirit to shape your view of what God's Word says. I plead with you to do it for the sake of not only your marriage but also the sake of the marriages that are headed toward suicide.

Your devotions and assignments for the week are as follows:

DAY 1:

Read Genesis 2 and answer the following questions.

- How difficult was life for Adam by himself? Give personal illustrations.
- What were God's specific directions for the design of marriage?

DAY 2:

Read Ephesians 5 and answer the following questions.

- Write out the expectations God has for the wife in marriage.
- Write out the expectations God has for the husband in marriage.

DAY 3:

Read Song of Solomon 1-4 and answer the following questions.

- Describe God's view of intimacy. Be specific in your responses:
- Describe how you are able to safeguard your marriage from intimacy-breakers.

DAY 4:

Read Song of Solomon 5-8 and answer the following questions.

- Describe God's view concerning sex.
- Describe God's role in intimacy. What does He think about intimacy, and what types of intimacy does He bless?

DAY 5:

Read 1 Peter 3 and answer the following questions.

- Describe the hardest part of being a witness to a lost spouse.
- Interact with 1 Peter 3:8 and come up with a game plan for how to successfully pray together as a couple. Write down the plan.

WEEK THIRTY-ONE
Doing the Wrong Thing

Scripture focus: Mark 10:13-16

And they were bringing children to Him so that He might touch them; but the disciples rebuked them. But when Jesus saw this, He was indignant and said to them, "Permit the children to come to Me; do not hinder them; for the kingdom of God belongs to such as these. Truly I say to you, whoever does not receive the kingdom of God like a child will not enter it at all." And He took them in His arms and began blessing them, laying His hands on them (NASB).

There Jesus is--we see Him in the house. There's so much to be done. People are constantly coming and needing ministry. Jesus' teaching and His touch are so vital to the work of the Kingdom. As He ministers we also see the ministry of the apprentices, who oversee crowd control. They often find themselves making decisions about who Jesus is to see and from whom they are to protect Him.

In this scene we visualize mothers, fathers, grandparents, aunts and uncles, and older siblings each bringing children to Jesus so that He might pray a prayer of blessing over these children. In the moment the apprentices, as is the case with me from time to time, "did the wrong thing."

The apprentices were preventing the children (possibly from infancy to preteen ages) from meeting Jesus. Mark's description of Jesus' response is strong. They were literally displeasing Jesus. This displeasure led to the strongest of rebukes as Jesus effectively said, "Stop preventing and start allowing these children to come to Me."

Before we get too deep into our discussion, I want you to get out of your mind two scenes:

- The scene of children running around totally off the chain in their reactions. They were not disrespectful or disruptive.

- The scene of children who were looking for selfish gain. They did not want to be blessed simply so they could get more and more for themselves. They were simply following the lead of others who said, "You need to meet Jesus."

With this clarified, we jump back into our study:

Jesus was longing for the children to come, while the apprentices were following the culture of the day, which basically implied that children were a hindrance without value. Such a culture was either pushing children away from God or was abusing them. The apprentices' view was that these children needed to wait until they were adults before they had value.

Jesus' view was just the opposite.

He shared with his apprentices about the importance of instructing children in how to be saved. He reminded them of how children offer the greatest illustration of how a person is to walk the path of faith and acceptance that leads to life in Jesus.

This teaching from Jesus strikes to the deepest core of my heart. It is so easy to get busy in an adult-driven world that we forget the importance of sharing and reaching children with the gospel. I remember back to my teenage days when my local church would engage in summer Bible clubs. These clubs were geared to share Jesus with children who had never heard. It was in these clubs where I first saw the gospel at work. Hundreds of children were changed through the gospel. It was here where I was taught the value God placed on children.

The children in those remote places in eastern Kentucky had little earthly future and no eternal hope apart from Jesus. But God so loved them that He sent His best, His only begotten Son to die for them. He also so loved them that He called His church to go to them with the message of hope and redemption. Therefore, we were there.

God created His kingdom for all the children of the world. This week you will be challenged in your reading to consider your heart toward the children of the world. It is my prayer that because of walking with the apprentices, you and I will gain a greater heart for the children of the world.

Here are our reading assignments for the week:

DAY 1:

Read Matthew 19:13-15 and Luke 18 and answer the following questions.

- Explain the difference between Jesus' view and the rich man's view of salvation.
- Can you identify more with the Pharisee or the tax collector in Luke 18:9-14? Explain.

DAY 2:

Read Ezekiel 2 and answer the following questions.
- What was God's view of the people of Israel?
- What was Ezekiel's view of the people?

DAY 3:

Read Provers 4 and answer the following questions.

- What is the father's role with his children according to this text?
- How difficult is it to get children to understand the Word of God in our day?

DAY 4:

Read 2 Samuel 14-15 and answer the following questions.

- What was David's view toward his children?
- How would you have handled the conflict if you were in David's place?

DAY 5:

Read Genesis 49 and answer the following questions.

- How well did Jacob know his sons, and how well do we know our sons and daughters?
- What blessings are you speaking over your children?

Coming Up Short

Scripture focus: Mark 10:17-31

As He was setting out on a journey, a man ran up to Him and knelt before Him, and asked Him, "Good Teacher, what shall I do to inherit eternal life?" And Jesus said to him, "Why do you call Me good? No one is good except God alone. You know the commandments, 'DO NOT MURDER, DO NOT COMMIT ADULTERY, DO NOT STEAL, DO NOT BEAR FALSE WITNESS, DO NOT DEFRAUD, HONOR YOUR FATHER AND MOTHER.'" And he said to Him, "Teacher, I have kept all these things from my youth up." Looking at him, Jesus felt a love for him and said to him, "One thing you lack: go and sell all you possess and give to the poor, and you will have treasure in heaven; and come, follow Me." But at these words he was saddened, and he went away grieving, for he was one who owned much property.

And Jesus, looking around, said to His disciples, "How hard it will be for those who are wealthy to enter the kingdom of God!" The disciples were amazed at His words. But Jesus answered again and said to them, "Children, how hard it is to enter the kingdom of God! It is easier for a camel to go through the eye of a needle than for a rich man to enter the kingdom of God." They were even more astonished and said to Him, "Then who can be saved?" Looking at them, Jesus said, "With people it is impossible, but not with God; for all things are possible with God."

Peter began to say to Him, "Behold, we have left everything and followed You." Jesus said, "Truly I say to you, there is no one who has left house or brothers or sisters or mother or father or children or farms, for My sake and for the gospel's sake, but that he will receive a hundred times as much now in the present age, houses and brothers and sisters and mothers and children and farms, along with persecutions; and in the age to come, eternal life. But many who are first will be last, and the last, first" (NASB).

I remember those early days of my life that included living near my grandparents. They had a large farm of which all our family owned different parts. They also owned a small country store. I often spent time with my grandfather in the store. We could always buy what we wanted, because my dad always paid the bill. Sometimes I would notice other children coming to the store, some of whom would have a few pennies in one hand. They would ask for some small piece of candy. No matter how short they were in having what the candy cost, my grandfather would give them what they asked for. I was confused. I asked my grandfather, "Why do you give them what they ask? They always come up short on money." I still remember his response: "It's okay. I just give it to them."

Question: Is our salvation earned or is it a gift from God?

This is the question that dominates the landscape of this week's Scripture focus. Our apprentices have been reminded of the importance of children responding to the gospel. These children are amazing illustrations of the heart attitude one must have to be saved.

What happens next is included in Scripture because the Holy Spirit directed Mark to write about it. I imagine that as Peter shared the story of what happened, he must have been filled with great emotion. Such should always be the case when souls are on the line.

The Bible identifies the person who comes to Jesus as simply a man. However, church history has given him a title: "the rich young ruler." The story is of love. We see both the love of Jesus and the love of the rich man. He comes with a question: "What can I do to inherit eternal life?"

This is truly a question that is being answered by our society. Our society believes two things:

- Everyone must accept everyone's view concerning how they should live life.

- God must accept everyone's view concerning how they should live life.

This man comes and seeks Jesus' affirmation for his views. Jesus' response does not affirm him but seeks to awaken him to his false view. The man hears Jesus' view and responds with a view that seems to say, "I'm doing everything you say I'm to do." But a deeper look reveals something else.

Think about Jesus' love for this man. He essentially tells him, "You do not believe I am the Son of God." If he really believed Jesus was God, he would have said more than "You are a good man." This is the same view of another ruler in John 3.

Jesus also tells this man that the commandments cannot save him because he does not have the ability to live up to the commandments. Yes, in the man's mind he had perfectly kept the last six, which relate to loving others. But it was the first four, which relate to our loving God, that he could not keep.

The man loved money more than he loved God. His confidence was replaced by coldness as he considered having to give up what he loved. His focus moved from God to his gold. Mark says, "He went away sorrowful, for he had great possessions. The truth is, this man rejected Jesus because he was in love with money.

I wonder how many multitudes reject Jesus every day because of their love for something or someone else. This is a sobering encounter. Peter is in shock because this seems to be a good man. If good men can't be saved, then who can?

There's only one problem with this: there are zero good people except the God-Man, Jesus Christ. Therefore, we understand that all will come up short in trying to earn their salvation (see Romans 3:23).

But what is impossible with me is possible with God. All who respond to the gospel will be saved. All who reject the gospel will be eternally lost. This week your readings will focus on the great truths of salvation. May God grant us the joy of understanding it all.

Here are our assignments for the week:

DAY 1:

Read Matthew 22 and answer the following questions.

- What are the requirements for someone's being accepted into heaven?
- Why would someone seek to get into heaven on his or her own merits?

DAY 2:

Read Romans 8 and answer the following questions.

- Why are people condemned by God?
- Does God love all people or just the people who respond to His call of salvation?

DAY 3:

Read Genesis 15 and answer the following questions.

- What was Abraham's status before God when God spoke to him in this chapter?
- Why did God walk through the covenant all alone?

DAY 4:

Read Revelation 5 and answer the following questions.

- What does the scroll contain? Explain your answer.
- Why is Jesus described as the Lamb standing as though it had been slain?

DAY 5:

Read Acts 15 and answer the following questions.

- Why were these Jewish people convinced that they needed to be circumcised to be saved?
- What was the church's final answer concerning how a person is saved?

WEEK THIRTY-THREE

Life on the Road

Scripture focus: Mark 10:32-45

They were on the road going up to Jerusalem, and Jesus was walking on ahead of them; and they were amazed, and those who followed were fearful. And again He took the twelve aside and began to tell them what was going to happen to Him, saying, "Behold, we are going up to Jerusalem, and the Son of Man will be delivered to the chief priests and the scribes; and they will condemn Him to death and will hand Him over to the Gentiles. They will mock Him and spit on Him, and scourge Him and kill Him, and three days later He will rise again."

James and John, the two sons of Zebedee, came up to Jesus, saying, "Teacher, we want You to do for us whatever we ask of You." And He said to them, "What do you want Me to do for you?" They said to Him, "Grant that we may sit, one on Your right and one on Your left, in Your glory." But Jesus said to them, "You do not know what you are asking. Are you able to drink the cup that I drink, or to be baptized with the baptism with which I am baptized?" They said to Him, "We are able." And Jesus said to them, "The cup that I drink you shall drink; and you shall be baptized with the baptism with which I am baptized. But to sit on My right or on My left, this is not Mine to give; but it is for those for whom it has been prepared."

Hearing this, the ten began to feel indignant with James and John. Calling them to Himself, Jesus said to them, "You know that those who are recognized as rulers of the Gentiles lord it over them; and their great men exercise authority over them. But it is not this way among you, but whoever wishes to become great among you shall be your servant; and whoever wishes to be first among you shall be slave of all. For even the Son of Man did not come to be served, but to serve, and to give His life a ransom for many" (NASB).

The road of our lives takes many turns in a lifetime. For those of us who are on the narrow road (Matthew 7:13-14) it may seem as if the road is sometimes endless and unfair. But the truth is--we need every turn on the road.

You and I have been traveling with Jesus for thirty-three weeks on many different roads. For the third time Jesus takes us on the road of prophecy concerning the hour of His going to the Cross. By now it would seem certain that the guys would embrace this road. But once again the Cross was not in the proper place in their lives.

Question: Why does it take us so long to mature in our Christian life? Answer: There are a lot of rough edges that need to be knocked off our lives. It takes a while for us to see this.

I wonder as I hear Jesus speak about the Cross if these men were starting to sense that the road they are on is going to take a tough turn. When we look at Jesus we realize He has always been on this road (Ephesians 1:1-4). His has been a straight path heading toward our redemption.

Mark is clear: Jesus is the Son of Man. This is His identity with us. Jesus will be delivered over. This has always been His intention. Jesus will be mocked, spit upon, and killed. This has always been the investment Jesus has been willing to make.

Surely the apprentices have matured enough to ask questions here, but they do not ask questions. Instead, they move right into a selfish moment. Two brothers are seeking to be leaders in Jesus' kingdom to come.

In my life I can honestly say that there have been times when I was even more immature in my walk with Christ. When I was in my twenties I was arrogant as I thought I knew everything and had the world by the tail. When I was in my thirties I was striving to lead the top of the success charts. In my forties I began to discover that greatness comes through humility, service, and obedience. Just like the other apprentices, I would hear Mark 10:45 and totally miss the truth of it.

Take a moment and see yourself with James and John. I see myself there. Both guys believe they can stand as Jesus is standing. These guys do not realize the truth of the Cross. Jesus is going to the Cross to suffer rejection, to die the most violent of deaths, and to purchase our forgiveness. These men could die and be rejected by men, but their efforts would not purchase anyone's forgiveness.

Both these guys would suffer, and both would give their lives in God's service. But the Cross was Christ's alone to bear.

This week I have chosen five Scriptures that I believe will challenge you regarding the life circumstances you have encountered. Please take the time to really place yourself in each passage. Struggle with the passage and dissect each verse with the goal of discovering God's purpose for your being on the road in each of those moments.

Here are our assignments for the week:

DAY 1:

Read Acts 12 and answer the following questions.

- What benefit could there possibly be in a Christian being killed?
- How would you pray for the person who kills someone without reason?

DAY 2:

Read Romans 8 and answer the following questions.

- Explain how Romans 8 gives perspective to life's toughest moments.
- How do we know God really loves us?

DAY 3:

Read Matthew 20 and answer the following questions.

- Why were the other apprentices angry with James and John?
- What would you ask Jesus if you had a personal and private audience with Him?

DAY 4:

Read 1 Samuel 15 and answer the following questions.

- Did Saul really commit a sin that merited his being removed from the throne of Israel?
- Why was Saul's sin so significant in his day and in what ways do we commit this sin in our day?

DAY 5:

Read James 4 and answer the following questions.

- What did James believe caused the greatest turmoil in a person's life? Explain.
- According to James 4:13-17 making assumptions can be a dangerous move. How should we approach each day?

WEEK THIRTY-FOUR

Making the Correct Call

Scripture focus: Mark 10:46-52

Then they came to Jericho. And as He was leaving Jericho with His disciples and a large crowd, a blind beggar named Bartimaeus, the son of Timaeus, was sitting by the road. When he heard that it was Jesus the Nazarene, he began to cry out and say, "Jesus, Son of David, have mercy on me!" Many were sternly telling him to be quiet, but he kept crying out all the more, "Son of David, have mercy on me!" And Jesus stopped and said, "Call him here." So they called the blind man, saying to him, "Take courage, stand up! He is calling for you." Throwing aside his cloak, he jumped up and came to Jesus. And answering him, Jesus said, "What do you want Me to do for you?" And the blind man said to Him, "Rabboni, I want to regain my sight!" And Jesus said to him, "Go; your faith has made you well." Immediately he regained his sight and began following Him on the road (NASB).

Years ago I was asked by one of our church members to help him out of a tough spot. He simply wanted me to umpire the end of a tee-ball game that he was unable to finish the night before.

I thought it would be easy. No big deal because it was just a game. Little did I know until I got there that it was a playoff game. All was going well until a close call turned everything into turmoil.

When the world was created by God, everything was going well--until Adam rebelled against God. From that moment the world was thrust into turmoil. We see the turmoil in the life of one man. His name was Bartimaeus. His turmoil? He was a blind beggar.

Brothers and sisters, every person has both a name and a problem. This man's earthly problem was blindness, and his eternal problem was sin. Jesus came to meet both needs.

The Bible says, "Bartimaeus . . . was sitting by the road" (NASB). Here we see him in his usual place. He has embraced his broken status and is among other broken people (Matthew 20:29-34). Suddenly he hears the noise of a crowd coming and asks, "What's happening?" Someone says, "It's Jesus of Nazareth."

In this moment the blind man is about to make a call--not a baseball call or a phone call, but an eternal call. He cries out, "Jesus, Son of David, have mercy on me!" Brothers and sisters, let me ask you a question: Was this the correct call? Yes indeed. This blind man could see better than most in that massive crowd.

He has come to know what King David came to know. He has come to know what every person who makes the correct eternal call knows. He knows Jesus is the Son of God, who has come to be the Messiah of the world. He knows that Jesus has all power, and he knows that if Jesus chooses to extend mercy, he could have his sight restored.

Question: Are you making the right eternal calls? There are people all around you who are broken. The Bible says that the people in the crowd told the man to be quiet. But he would not be quiet. I wonder: are we by our actions telling people to be quiet? When Jesus hears this man, He calls him to come to Him.

The man does three amazing things:

- He throws off his overcoat as a sign that he is about to break with his old way of life.

- He springs up in full faith believing he is about to be made whole.

- He comes to Jesus because he knows Jesus is the only way of life.

The scene that follows is filled with correct calls. Jesus asks the man, "What do you want me to do for you?" The man makes the correct call: "I want my sight restored." Romans 10:13 tells us of the richness of God's mercy in saving all who call on Him. Jesus heals the man instantly. The man's faith is rewarded with sight. Bartimaeus makes one more correct call: he follows Jesus.

This man's life is forever changed by the correct calls! This week I want to challenge you to think about the many calls you have made when it comes to your own life and the lives of people you have encountered over the years. Someone said that on average, ninety percent of the people we meet will never hear the good news of the gospel. Brothers and sisters, may this never be said of us. Let's make the correct calls for the glory of God. This week you will be studying scriptures that will help you to make the correct calls.

Here are our assignments for the week:

DAY 1:

Read Romans 10 and answer the following questions.
- Why should every person know how to be saved? Explain.
- Why should every believer know how to lead someone to be saved?

DAY 2:

Read 2 Samuel 7 and answer the following questions.

- What had God done for David?
- What was God going to do for the world? Explain.

DAY 3:

Read 2 Corinthians 6 and answer the following questions.

- Why was Paul so urgent in his appeal at the beginning of this chapter?
- Is there an urgency, or a lack of urgency, in the church where you belong?

DAY 4:

Read 1 Peter 4 and answer the following questions.

- What changes does a person need to make when he or she says yes to Jesus?
- Why is it so important to share the gospel now and not later? Explain.

DAY 5:

Read 2 Kings 5 and answer the following questions.

- What role did the slave girl play in her master's healing?
- What role are you and I called to play in the lives of our neighbors? Explain.

When the Singing Starts

Scripture focus: Mark 11:1-11

*A*s *they approached Jerusalem and came to Bethphage and Bethan-yat the Mount of Olives, Jesus sent two of his disciples, saying to them, "Go to the village ahead of you, and just as you enter it, you will find a colt tied there, which no one has ever ridden. Untie it and bring it here. If anyone asks you, 'Why are you doing this?' say, 'The Lord needs it and will send it back here shortly.'"*

They went and found a colt outside in the street, tied at a doorway. As they untied it, some people standing there asked, "What are you doing, untying that colt?" They answered as Jesus had told them to, and the people let them go. When they brought the colt to Jesus and threw their cloaks over it, he sat on it. Many people spread their cloaks on the road, while others spread branches they had cut in the fields. Those who went ahead and those who followed shouted,

"Hosanna!"

"Blessed is he who comes in the name of the Lord!"

"Blessed is the coming kingdom of our father David!"

"Hosanna in the highest heaven!"

Jesus entered Jerusalem and went into the temple courts. He looked around at everything, but since it was already late, he went out to Bethany with the Twelve (NIV).

It happens every week. The pre-worship music fades out, and then we see the countdown beginning on the screens. It begins at eight, and then when the countdown hits zero we're ready for the announcements of the church. At the end our announcer usually says, "Now it's time for worship."

Pastor Cary steps onto the platform and says, "Welcome to worship today." Question: How often are you and I prepared to worship the Lord? Be honest--God knows. Each week God wants us to be truly ready and to genuinely worship Him.

I believe there are three types of worshipers in our church each week:

- There are those who truly worship. We see them coming to worship the God they have been worshiping all week.

- There are those who are trying to worship. I see them with tears in my eyes because I know they're facing life's toughest moments, and they're still saying, "I love You, Lord, and I trust You."

- There are those who pretend to worship. Life is all about them. We see these people in our Scripture focus.

Go back with me to the time of the first apprentices. Walk with me in those days when the apprentices were in Jesus' presence each day. Were they prepared each day to worship Jesus? Were they truly worshipers, trying worshipers, or were they simply pretending to worship?

Jesus has left Jericho and is following His divinely appointed GPS, which says "Jerusalem." The time of the year is the week before Passover. Passover is the day when all of Israel looks back to the moment when her people were delivered from bondage (Exodus 12). But at the same time this day is a celebration of hope for the people. They believe that the true Lamb of God will someday come to deliver Israel from her enemies. When Messiah comes, Israel will be redeemed.

Little did the people know that Messiah was coming to Jerusalem on this Passover. The original apprentices are still coming to understand all of this. Presently they are dealing with the bomb shell delivered by Jesus. On three occasions He has said, "I am going to Jerusalem; I will be betrayed, beaten, crucified, and buried; and three days later I will come out of the grave." When we consider this, we would have to place the apprentices in the category of "trying worshipers."

The truth is that you and I are sometimes "trying worshipers." Question: What usually occupies your mind as you make your way to worship? The list could be long for us. Here are a few: finances, family issues, work assignments, health issues, scheduling conflicts, or What am I going to do my class project on? These mind-consuming matters along with hundreds more keep us locked into our lives, which often are void of heaven's direction. As hard as we may try, we just can't seem to worship. Let's look back at the apprentices.

This day is filled with action, but it begins with worship. The apprentices are told to go and borrow a donkey, and they are to bring it to Jesus. Jesus gets on the donkey and begins being led into the city of Jerusalem.

Suddenly as they're making their way up the hill to Jerusalem, people begin shouting and singing. This is a big deal moment. I wonder if the apprentices are shocked by the worship of people who have been on the fence about Jesus. I wonder if the apprentices want to quiet the crowd. Do the apprentices join in the worship?

In this moment we look away from the apprentices and focus on the crowd and the context of what they're singing. First look at the crowd. We see them with sincere hope. This could be the Messiah. This could be the man who is going to reestablish the throne of David! This could be the one who will make us prosperous as a nation again. They seem to be truly worshiping.

The people cry out, "Lord, save!" They place their jackets on the path signifying that they are submitting to His Lordship. But five days later these same people will cry, "Crucify Him!"

Brothers and sisters, what happened? Answer: They were only pretending to worship Jesus. It was all about them.

What amazes me more than anything else about this passage is Jesus' kindness in accepting their worship. He does not rebuke them nor does He put them down. Yes, they were wrong. But after the Cross many of them would be saved.

This week take time to both examine the why of your worship as well as daily engaging in true worship of the King. I have placed each Psalm before you to help in this process.

Here are our assignments for the week:

DAY 1:
Read Psalm 113 and answer the following questions.
- What are some things God has graciously done for our world?
- What are the things the Psalmist lists as God's works in the world?

DAY 2:
Read Psalm 114 and answer the following questions.
- If you had been alive in Moses' day, how would you have praised the Lord, and what would you have praised Him for?
- What are the miracles you are asking God for this day?

DAY 3:

Read Psalm 115 and answer the following questions.

- Why do people tend to want to worship themselves or lesser gods?
- Why is it important for God to remember His people?

DAY 4:

Read Psalm 116 and answer the following questions.

- What does the Psalmist mean by "I will lift up the cup of salvation and call on the name of the LORD" (Psalm 116:13, NIV)?
- What does the Psalmist mean by "I will pay my vows to the LORD" (Psalm 116:14)?

DAY 5:

Read Psalm 117 and Psalm 118 and answer the following questions.

- Why is it better to take refuge in God?
- Where and why does the Psalmist refer to Jesus' ministry?

WEEK THIRTY-SIX

The Day Jesus Attended Church

Scripture focus: Mark 11:15-19

On reaching Jerusalem, Jesus entered the temple courts and began driving out those who were buying and selling there. He overturned the tables of the money changers and the benches of those selling doves, and would not allow anyone to carry merchandise through the temple courts. And as he taught them, he said, "Is it not written: 'My house will be called a house of prayer for all nations'? But you have made it 'a den of robbers.'" The chief priests and the teachers of the law heard this and began looking for a way to kill him, for they feared him, because the whole crowd was amazed at his teaching. When evening came, Jesus and his disciples went out of the city (NIV).

The city of Jerusalem was alive with activity and anticipation. It was Passover week. Literally hundreds of thousands of visitors had made the pilgrimage to this place to celebrate. Every hotel was full, boarding houses were overfilled, and all the guest bedrooms were overcrowded. Families had opened their homes. And to top it off, Jesus had come to town. I imagine the apprentices were stressed by all they were seeing. People were walking, taking, working, selling, arguing, and catching up.

But in the center of all of this was Jesus. On this day He enters the central building in the city, the place that had formerly stood as a light to the nations. This was the place where God used to meet with His people. But now it was only a temple made by human hands. What Jesus saw stirred Him in the deepest of ways.

Here are my observations of the moment:

- The chief priests under the authority of the High Priest have taken over God's house.

God ordained that His house would be the place where He would meet with His people. Leviticus 1-7 teaches us of the grace and mercy of God in creating a place where the people could come to have their sins dealt with on the altar of sacrifice. But now it is merely an empty ritual because God is no longer there.

- The chief priests under the authority of the High priest have turned God's house into a place of earthly profit.

The leaders are charging people outrageous prices to buy the required sacrifices. The Temple accepts only Jewish currency, so all other has to be exchanged at mafia prices.

The people who are coming for help find more burdens. They are having to participate in corrupt practices and thus are still under the wrath of God. The fact is--it was a useless trip.

Question: "Does the church have value when you attend?" The church must be a place where hurting people can come and freely hear about God with no distractions. The church must be a people who are seeking to bring others to Jesus.

As I read this I wonder, What did the apprentices think about Jesus' actions? It would be later when Peter would understand as well as the other disciples. Be assured that there are things that happen in church that seem to be disasters but turn out to be our defining moments.

Jim Cymbala writes about this in his book God's Grace from Ground Zero. Jim shares about how his church and so many other churches opened their doors to the broken, the battered, and the rescue personnel who did their best to save thousands of lives. That disaster moment was a defining moment for the community to truly see God's heart for all people.

In our focal text Jesus takes back God's house, turning a broken place into a place of blessing for five days. In those days Jesus teaches in the Temple. The glory has returned. In those days Jesus heals people and leads people to true salvation. The Temple has never been so bright.

I want you to consider this truth: "When the people of God are living as they should, the place where they worship God becomes a miracle place where Jesus is at work."

I want you to consider this truth: "Jesus is to be the Lord of the church." We should not have to be wondering if He is coming. We should expect His coming, and we should not move without His coming.

This week you will interact with scripture that will help you understand Jesus' work in His church as well as what our responsibilities are regarding the church. Lord, move in Your church and Your people this week.

Here are our assignments for the week:

DAY 1:

Read Matthew 21 and answer the following questions.

- Who are the blind and lame in our city, and where do they go for help?
- Why were the chief priests and scribes so upset with the people who were giving praise to Jesus?

DAY 2:

Read 1 Corinthians 6 and answer the following questions.

- What type of problems do most churches have that could be solved if Jesus were the Lord of the church?
- What should be the church's position toward unconfessed sin in the church?

DAY 3:

Read Luke 19 and answer the following questions.

- Why was Jesus weeping over the city of Jerusalem?
- Describe what Sunday might look like if Jesus were the teacher.

DAY 4:

Read Revelation 2 and answer the following questions.

- What happened to the church at Ephesus?
- What type of church was the church at Thyatira?

DAY 5:

Read Revelation 3 and answer the following questions.

- How do Jesus' words to the church at Philadelphia encourage you?
- Is there any hope for the church of Laodicea? If so, explain.

Don't Blame the Fruit

Scripture focus: Mark 11:12-14, 20-25

The next day as they were leaving Bethany, Jesus was hungry. Seeing in the distance a fig tree in leaf, he went to find out if it had any fruit. When he reached it, he found nothing but leaves, because it was not the season for figs. Then he said to the tree, "May no one ever eat fruit from you again." And his disciples heard him say it.

In the morning, as they went along, they saw the fig tree withered from the roots. Peter remembered and said to Jesus, "Rabbi, look! The fig tree you cursed has withered!" . . .

"Have faith in God," Jesus answered. "Truly I tell you, if anyone says to this mountain, 'Go, throw yourself into the sea,' and does not doubt in their heart but believes that what they say will happen, it will be done for them. Therefore I tell you, whatever you ask for in prayer, believe that you have received it, and it will be yours. And when you stand praying, if you hold anything against anyone, forgive them, so that your Father in heaven may forgive you your sins" (NIV).

"This water tastes terrible!" These words came from both boys as they took the first drink of water from the family well. They had always enjoyed the water, but this time it was different. The father decided that the boys were correct. He looked into the well and discovered what had happened. A squirrel had fallen into it and died.

Question: Was this the fault of the water or the squirrel?

As we come to our focal text of the week we read of a very strange occurrence in the ministry of Jesus. Jesus pronounces a curse on a fig tree. The Bible records Jesus looking for fruit on the tree. When He does not find it, the tree is done for.

I can honestly say that this is a hard passage to grasp. It must have been hard for the apprentices. In every place they had traveled Jesus had repeatedly blessed those He encountered. But here came the opposite.

When you look closely at the content you discover how often Jesus referred to Israel as being choice fruit in the Old Testament. In Jeremiah 24 we see Israel divided into both good fruit and bad fruit. The question that comes to mind is this: What causes fruit to be either good or bad? Answer: Don't blame the fruit. The fruit is simply what comes from the source of its life.

Israel found its life in its religion and its connection to the Temple. On the previous day Jesus turned the activities in the Temple on edge. The cursing of the fig tree points us to two things:

- This is a picture of Israel's system of religion. "It's over."
- This is a portrait of Israel's life apart from faith in Jesus Christ. "There is no good fruit."

On the next morning when the apprentices come back into the city of Jerusalem, Peter spots the fig tree. Do you see it? The leaves are gone, the branches and trunk are rotten and brittle. There is no life.

Less than twenty-four hours earlier there was life. But at the Word of Jesus, it was dead.

Peter is amazed at this moment. He points out to Jesus the great miracle. Jesus responds: "Have faith in God." Peter believes it. Both blessing and cursing come from God. Peter will need this mountain-moving type faith in God as he and the other apprentices face those who have both dead religion and depravity of life.

The disciples will need to focus not on the fruit of dead religion and depravity but on the root of the problem. Life could come only through faith in Jesus Christ (Philippians 3:9). Life in Christ produces fruit that is bold, courageous, and confident (Ephesians 3:12) even in the presence of towering mountains.

As Jesus completes His teaching in this section, we read the following: "Whenever you stand praying, forgive, if you have anything against anyone, so that your Father who is in heaven will also forgive you your transgressions" (Mark 11:25, NASB).

Faith produces such fruit that includes a heart that forgives. If we are going to bear good fruit we must have a clear connection to Jesus. If we have unforgiveness in our hearts, we have an obstruction that keeps the life of Jesus from flowing to the fruit of our lives. The Temple had become simply a dead religious place because the people had no life. The temple of our lives can be fruitless when there is an obstruction. I pray that the Lord bears great fruit in our lives this week as we look deeper than the fruit to the source of either good or bad fruit.

Here are our assignments for the week:

DAY 1:

Read Jeremiah 24 and answer the following questions.
- Describe the two types of fruit referred to in these chapters.
- What happens to the good fruit and the bad fruit?

DAY 2:

Read Joel 2 and answer the following questions.

- What does it mean to return to the Lord with all your heart?
- Has Israel returned to the Lord? Give reasons to defend your answer.

DAY 3:

Read Revelation 7 and answer the following questions.

- Who are the 144,000?
- Who are the great multitudes, and why are they praising the Lord?

DAY 4:

Read Romans 9 and answer the following questions.

- Is there a different way for Israel to be saved.
- Who is the true Israel?

DAY 5:

Read Matthew 21 and answer the following questions.

- Where does faith come into the production of good and bad fruit?
- What role does faith play in your fruit-bearing?

WEEK THIRTY-EIGHT

This is About You

Scripture focus: Mark 12:1-17

*J*esus then began to speak to them in parables: "A man planted a vineyard. He put a wall around it, dug a pit for the winepress and built
*a watchtower. Then he rented the vineyard to some farmers and moved to
another place. At harvest time he sent a servant to the tenants to collect
from them some of the fruit of the vineyard. But they seized him, beat him
and sent him away empty-handed. Then he sent another servant to them;
they struck this man on the head and treated him shamefully. He sent still
another, and that one they killed. He sent many others; some of them they
beat, others they killed.*

"*He had one left to send, a son, whom he loved. He sent him last of all,
saying, 'They will respect my son.'*

"*But the tenants said to one another, 'This is the heir. Come, let's kill
him, and the inheritance will be ours.' So they took him and killed him,
and threw him out of the vineyard.*

"*What then will the owner of the vineyard do? He will come and kill
those tenants and give the vineyard to others. Haven't you read this passage
of Scripture:*

"'The stone the builders rejected
has become the cornerstone;
the Lord has done this,
and it is marvelous in our eyes'?"

Then the chief priests, the teachers of the law and the elders looked for a way to arrest him because they knew he had spoken the parable against them. But they were afraid of the crowd; so they left him and went away.

Later they sent some of the Pharisees and Herodians to Jesus to catch him in his words. They came to him and said, "Teacher, we know that you are a man of integrity. You aren't swayed by others, because you pay no attention to who they are; but you teach the way of God in accordance with the truth. Is it right to pay the imperial tax to Caesar or not? Should we pay or shouldn't we?"

But Jesus knew their hypocrisy. "Why are you trying to trap me?" he asked. "Bring me a denarius and let me look at it." They brought the coin, and he asked them, "Whose image is this? And whose inscription?"

"Caesar's," they replied.

Then Jesus said to them, "Give back to Caesar what is Caesar's and to God what is God's."

And they were amazed at him (NIV).

This week's Scripture focus must be approached with the keenest of spiritual eyes. The truth of it is explosive for our personal lives. If you haven't already noticed, I've entitled this week's focus as "This Is About You."

The ministry of Jesus is coming to its climactic point. The Cross is just days away. Jesus' teaching is becoming increasingly intense. The opposition's attacks are becoming more and more volatile. Their challenges to Jesus are becoming bolder (Mark 11:27). The goal of the opposition is simple: they are going to trap Jesus so they can terminate Him.

Here we see Jesus in the Temple. The apprentices are by His side. Two kingdom forces are standing on the field of battle. We see the kingdom of God led by King Jesus. We see the kingdom of humanity led by the religious leaders. In thirty short years from this time, Rome would march into Jerusalem establishing who was in charge of the people.

Jesus shares a story in the form of a parable. A parable is a story laid beside a truth that illustrates the truth. The truth is that Israel was established by God to be a nation that honored Him. The nation walked away from God. God sent prophet after prophet to turn them around. However, they refused to turn around, and they turned on God's prophets, beating some and killing others.

Now Jesus has come, but they will kill Him, seeking to take the kingdom for themselves. In Matthew's account of this moment it is clear: "This is about you." The religious leaders knew it but were unwilling to admit it or to repent of it.

Brothers and sisters, do we see ourselves in the story? The truth is we are all in the story.

- We were born into the kingdom of humanity (Ephesians 2:12-14).

As a member of this kingdom we wanted to live life as the king of our own castles. We desired to take everything for ourselves. We would not listen to anyone who told us otherwise. We were responsible for the death of God's Son.

- We need to be born again for another kingdom, the kingdom of God (Ephesians 2:15-17).

Jesus came so that we could be delivered from the kingdom of humanity. The question is--Have you changed kingdoms? Or could it be that you are trying to live part time in each? The people in Jeremiah's day wanted to keep their status in God's kingdom, but at the same time they wanted to enjoy the pleasures of the kingdom of humanity.

The prophets told of a day when Messiah would come. He would be crucified. He would rise from the grave. He would ascend to the Father. He would someday return to rule and reign.

The question comes: Have we aligned with His kingdom rule? The writer of 1 Peter speaks deeply about this issue in (1 Peter 2:4-10). Take time this week to consider your personal response to God's call to His kingdom. Take time to think prophetically concerning our day. Finally, take time to consider what you are willing to endure to walk as a citizen of God's kingdom.

Here are our assignments for the week:

DAY 1:
Read Isaiah 5 and answer the following questions.
- Why did God break down the walls around Israel's vineyard?
- What implications does this text have for our day?

DAY 2:
Read Psalm 80 and answer the following questions.
- Is God angry with the church? Explain your answer.
- What must happen so that America can be right with God?

DAY 3:
Read Psalm 81 and answer the following questions.
- Why does God want His people to listen to Him?
- What hope does this psalm offer you personally?

DAY 4:
Read Jeremiah 37 and 38 and answer the following questions.
- Why was it life-threating for Jeremiah to share the truth?
- Describe what it must have felt like for Jeremiah to sink in the mud.

DAY 5:

Read Luke 20 and answer the following questions.

- Where did Jesus' authority come from?
- Why were the religious leaders shocked by what Jesus said (verse 17)?

WEEK THIRTY-NINE

The Imprints in Your Life

Scripture focus: Mark 12:13-17

Later they sent some of the Pharisees and Herodians to Jesus to catch him in his words. They came to him and said, "Teacher, we know that you are a man of integrity. You aren't swayed by others, because you pay no attention to who they are; but you teach the way of God in accordance with the truth. Is it right to pay the imperial tax to Caesar or not? Should we pay or shouldn't we?"

But Jesus knew their hypocrisy. "Why are you trying to trap me?" he asked. "Bring me a denarius and let me look at it." They brought the coin, and he asked them, "Whose image is this? And whose inscription?"

"Caesar's," they replied.

Then Jesus said to them, "Give back to Caesar what is Caesar's and to God what is God's."

And they were amazed at him (NIV).

As the hours counted down to the moment when Jesus would be betrayed, the atmosphere must have been getting more and more difficult. The forces of hell were gathering with the intent of stopping Jesus once and for all. You could see the imprints on every street corner. If you stopped by a blacksmith shop the older guys were standing around debating about what was going to happen. Down by the Pool of Bethesda the crowds of invalids were hoping that Jesus would come by and see them maybe one more time before the religious and political machine shut Him down.

In some ways the apprentices probably were wondering what would happen when things came to a head. Jesus had told them three times that He was going to the Cross. But somehow it seemed an impossibility for the one who had healed so many, taught so many, and even raised the dead.

These men were not who they used to be. The imprint of the gospel was clearly on their lives. But in these moments all eyes were on Jesus!

Read the next sentence very carefully: All your friends have their eyes on you during this time of uncertainty in America. The question for the week is this: What type of imprint do people see in your life?

It is not just during times of uncertainty in the country that people pay close attention to your life. They're watching all the time. For this reason, and also because the enemy is always at work, it is very important to be marked deeply by Christ.

We see this in Jesus' life. Mark records a moment that many just look past as not very important. But if it is in the Word of God it is important. The Bible says that a strange group comes to Jesus with a trap in the form of a question. The strangeness of the group lies is in the fact that they did not get along. The Herodians were the political friends of Herod. The Pharisees were the religious experts of Judaism. In this moment they come together against their common enemy, Jesus.

They make three statements about Jesus that they do not believe, but they are true:

- Jesus, You are a man of principle who is not swayed by opinion.
- Jesus, You teach the way of the Lord correctly.
- Jesus, You are a teacher.

The strange group has one question: "Is it correct to pay taxes to Rome?" Now taxes were an everyday part of Israel's political and religious DNA. Each year there were many Temple taxes and many Roman taxes to pay. But one particular question on a particular tax is on their minds now: Is it right to pay taxes that fund the rule of Caesar?

This was a powerful question: If Jesus responded "yes," then the religious crowd would turn on Him. If He responded, "no," then the government would turn on Him.

Notice the wisdom, wit, and the truth given by Jesus:

"Give to man what is required, and give to God what is required."

Brothers and sisters, this is amazing. The strange group did not expect this. I promise you that they went away frustrated. It can be that way sometimes in our lives as well--especially when we want to walk the middle-of-the-road path where we enjoy both the world and Christ.

Some look at this passage and conclude, I must pay my taxes, but I don't have to like it. Others conclude, I will do whatever I can to avoid paying, but if I have no other option, I'll do it. Still some have the correct view: When Christ has impacted your life, the imprints will lead you to give everything to God for His direction.

Be assured that God will direct you to pay your taxes and to pay your tithe. This week you will be asked to read five passages that will take you deeply into what is imprinted on your heart. If you find things that you do not like, it's not as if they can't be removed and overcome. Be ready to be imprinted by Jesus!

Here are our assignments for the week:

DAY 1:

Read John 13 and answer the following questions.

- Why is it important to have the image of Christ in your life?
- Why is love such a distinguishing mark of a true Christ-follower in our society? Do non-Christians love in a different way?

DAY 2:

Read Exodus 30 and answer the following questions.

- What was the purpose in the census tax?
- Would the church's finances be better if we collected taxes instead of tithes?

DAY 3:

Read Romans 14 and answer the following questions.

- How would the government view our faith if we refused to pay taxes?
- Was the American Revolution correct in its view of "no taxation without representation?"

DAY 4:

Read Titus 3 and answer the following questions.

- How does paying your taxes reflect the image of Christ?
- What does Paul mean by "be ready to whatever is good"?

DAY 5:

Read I John 2 and answer the following questions.

- What imprints does the gospel make on people's lives today?
- What imprints does the world make on people's lives today?

The Trouble with Being Wrong

Scripture focus: Mark 12:18-27

*T*hen the Sadducees, who say there is no resurrection, came to him with a question. "Teacher," they said, "Moses wrote for us that if a man's brother dies and leaves a wife but no children, the man must marry the widow and raise up offspring for his brother. Now there were seven brothers. The first one married and died without leaving any children. The second one married the widow, but he also died, leaving no child. It was the same with the third. In fact, none of the seven left any children. Last of all, the woman died too. At the resurrection whose wife will she be, since the seven were married to her?"*

Jesus replied, "Are you not in error because you do not know the Scriptures or the power of God? When the dead rise, they will neither marry nor be given in marriage; they will be like the angels in heaven. Now about the dead rising—have you not read in the Book of Moses, in the account of the burning bush, how God said to him, 'I am the God of Abraham, the God of Isaac, and the God of Jacob'? He is not the God of the dead, but of the living. You are badly mistaken!" (NIV).

Question: Have you ever been wrong? Be careful--your answer could be looked at by someone else. Sometimes there are moments when being wrong has little effect on the direction of one's life. For example, whether you take the shortest GPS route or the second shortest, usually the time will be about the same.

However, there are other moments when a person can greatly affect the direction of his or her life by being wrong--for example, how one responds to the text before us.

By this moment the apprentices must be wearing down with the constant traffic flow of individuals and groups of people who all thought they knew more than Jesus. The apprentices could not point the finger because they had also, from time to time, tried to correct Jesus.

Did that last sentence strike a nerve with you? It did me. Who in his or her right mind would ever try to correct the Son of God?

Mark has written about the meetings Jesus has had with the following groups:

- The Pharisees, who thought they knew more than Jesus.

- The Herodians, who also thought they knew more than Jesus.

- Now the Sadducees, who also thought they knew more than Jesus.

Who were the Sadducees? These were the small group of people who made up the Jewish political machine. The high priestly family usually would be a part of this group. Many writers have commented that these were the materialistic leaders of the day.

One of the major points of contention they had with Jesus was His teaching concerning the resurrection. They rejected this teaching altogether.

These leaders come with a question. Take time to read the whole question, which presumes a belief that God allows polygamy in heaven. Jesus patiently waits for the Sadducees to complete their teaching. Then He drops the hammer:

Jesus says, "There is no marriage in heaven."

Why? Keep in mind that purpose of marriage on earth is to be fruitful and multiply. In heaven this will be no longer needed because death will no longer exist. In heaven all citizens will be "children of the resurrection."

Jesus says, "He is the God of the living." This means that there will be a resurrection for those who die in Him. In this week's readings you will be asked to dig deeply into what this means. You will also be asked to come to a place of a settled viewpoint concerning this subject.

Why is it so important to get this right? The first subject Jesus spoke about was marriage. It's okay to get it wrong about marriage in heaven. You can still go to heaven through Jesus. But the second subject is one that you cannot be wrong about. If there is no resurrection then we are still lost, and we are doomed for eternity in hell. See 1 Corinthians 15:20 for a strong statement of hope.

Jesus closes the meeting with these strong words: "Ye therefore do greatly err" (KJV).

They were off the path. They were deceived. They were seriously wrong. If these political leaders kept on the same path, they really would each become "sad, you see." Check out John 14:1-6. Brothers and sisters, we cannot afford to get this wrong.

Here are our assignments for the week:

DAY 1:

Read Deuteronomy 25 and answer the following questions.
- What was the purpose in directing the widow to marry only within the family of her deceased husband?
- What will happen to our marriages in heaven?

DAY 2:

Read Exodus 3 and answer the following questions.

- Why did Jesus choose Moses' statement in Exodus 3 as His Old Testament text to prove the doctrine of the resurrection?
- How did this statement encourage Moses? Explain your answer.

DAY 3:

Read Job 19 and answer the following questions.

- What leads to a person deciding that he or she wants to die?
- What did Job know about our Redeemer?

DAY 4:

Read Psalm 16 and answer the following questions.

- What happens to our souls when we die?
- Explain "the path of life" (verse 11).

DAY 5:

Read Psalm 73 and answer the following questions.

- What is more important--heaven now or heaven in the hereafter?
- Why did the Psalmist desire to be with the Lord? See verse 25.

When Being Right is Not Enough

Scripture focus: Mark 12:28-34

*O*ne *of the teachers of the law came and heard them debating. Noticing that Jesus had given them a good answer, he asked him, "Of all the commandments, which is the most important?"*

"The most important one," answered Jesus, "is this: 'Hear, O Israel: The Lord our God, the Lord is one. Love the Lord your God with all your heart and with all your soul and with all your mind and with all your strength.' The second is this: 'Love your neighbor as yourself.' There is no command-ment greater than these."

"Well said, teacher," the man replied. "You are right in saying that God is one and there is no other but him. To love him with all your heart, with all your understanding and with all your strength, and to love your neigh-bor as yourself is more important than all burnt offerings and sacrifices."

When Jesus saw that he had answered wisely, he said to him, "You are not far from the kingdom of God." And from then on no one dared ask him any more questions (NIV).

It was now time for the heavy hitters to come at Jesus with their questions. Who were these heavy hitters? They were keepers of the law of God. They were to pass down from generation to generation the truth of God's Word.

Before us is the question of one scribe. We are not given his name, but we are told that he is impressed by Jesus' ability to articulate the Law. He acknowledges that Jesus has been teaching the truth.

So instead of trying to trap Jesus in a third-tear question, he goes directly to a first-tear question. It is a top of the spiritual food chain question: "What is the greatest commandment?"

Jesus again returns to the teaching of the Law in the Old Testament (Deuteronomy 6:4-5). The first commandment is to love God with all your heart, soul, mind, and strength. In the scribe's mind Jesus is spot on.

Once again Jesus quotes from the Old Testament (Leviticus 19:18). The second commandment is to love your neighbor as yourself. It could be put like this: Love your neighbor just as you love yourself.

Notice the strange turn of events: The scribe is very unusual in that he understands the greater value of loving God than offering useless sacrifices to God. He ia right on target in his understanding of God's emphasis on loving others. Without a doubt he has seen thousands of sacrifices from people who did not have a heart for God. He has also seen them mistreat their neighbors while all the while saying, "I know God."

Jesus acknowledges that this man has a right understanding of what kingdom life is all about. He makes a revealing statement that this man is not far from the kingdom of God. But apparently that's as far as it goes.

Right in front of this man is Jesus, the door into the kingdom (John 14:6). Here is Jesus, the one who knows the condition of the scribe's heart. In this moment I believe Jesus is presenting the invitation to this man. He wanted him to repent and to follow Him.

Did the man follow Jesus? We're not told in the text. But we do have some inside information from Matthew 22:34-40. Apparently the scribe was attempting to test Jesus' understanding of the Law. But now the tables were turned. Would this man follow Jesus?

Sadly, we are never told in Scripture if he did. I wonder--do you know the truth of Jesus? Recently I met a man who was a heavy drinker. As I began witnessing to him, it was clear that he knew the Bible. He quoted more verses than I did in our conversation. I was no better than he in the conversation. I later discovered that he was a pastor's son. But there was one sad thing missing from his life--he did not know Jesus! Make sure you know Jesus. Make sure that all who are around you know Jesus. This week's assignments will help you on the journey.

Here are our assignments for the week:

DAY 1:

Read Leviticus 19 and answer the following questions.
- Who did God consider to be Israel's neighbor?
- Who are your neighbors? What do you know about them?

DAY 2:

Read Deuteronomy 6 and answer the following questions.
- What does it mean to love God with all your heart, soul, and mind?
- What would a person's life look like if he or she were one hundred percent in love with God?

DAY 3:

Read Matthew 25 and answer the following questions.

- Whom is the Lord coming for? Explain.
- Will the scribes be on the left or the right on Judgment Day?

DAY 4:

Read Hebrews 6 and answer the following questions.

- Had the scribes in Mark 12 tasted the heavenly gift?
- Does a person have another chance after rejecting Jesus?

DAY 5:

Read Revelation 3 and answer the following questions.

- What does it mean to have a reputation of being alive?
- Why does Jesus stand at the door of people's hearts and simply knock?

The Hypocrite Syndrome

Scripture focus: Mark 12:35-44

While Jesus was teaching in the temple courts, he asked, "Why do the teachers of the law say that the Messiah is the son of David? David himself, speaking by the Holy Spirit, declared:

> *"'The Lord said to my Lord:*
> *"Sit at my right hand*
> *until I put your enemies*
> *under your feet."'*

David himself calls him 'Lord.' How then can he be his son?"
The large crowd listened to him with delight.

As he taught, Jesus said, "Watch out for the teachers of the law. They like to walk around in flowing robes and be greeted with respect in the marketplaces, and have the most important seats in the synagogues and the places of honor at banquets. They devour widows' houses and for a show make lengthy prayers. These men will be punished most severely."

Jesus sat down opposite the place where the offerings were put and watched the crowd putting their money into the temple treasury. Many rich people threw in large amounts. But a poor widow came and put in two very small copper coins, worth only a few cents.

Calling his disciples to him, Jesus said, "Truly I tell you, this poor widow has put more into the treasury than all the others. They all gave out of their wealth; but she, out of her poverty, put in everything—all she had to live on" (NIV).

Now that the questions had ceased, Jesus alone was speaking. The apprentices had to be on overload at this point. What would He say? The words of Jesus are both with warning and with strong urgency.

Jesus begins with an urgent quote from Psalm 110. He is proclaiming the fulfillment of this prophecy. The people respond with celebration as what they have been waiting for and longing for was coming to be.

Jesus cries out with love, "Beware . . ." Jesus has used this word before to communicate warnings, but in this moment he follows it up with a warning about a people. We know them to be scribes. But at a more base level, we would label them as hypocrites. Yes, you read it correctly. The scribes were struggling with the hypocrite syndrome.

Questions: Have you ever struggled with this syndrome? Do you know others who have or currently are struggling with this syndrome?

Jesus reveals the hidden secrets of such a syndrome:

- Such people outwardly want you to think they are righteous before God.
- Such people desire the outward respect of all people.
- Such people enjoy taking advantage of other people.
- Such people seem like godly people, but they are truly suffering from the hypocrite syndrome.

Let this sink in for a moment. How many people in our day pray but do not genuinely know the God they're praying to? How many lead in our churches and lead in our small groups but still do not know the Lord? They play in the band, go on mission trips, and hang out only with religious people, but still they are without Christ.

Here is shocking news: This syndrome dwells within every person at birth.

The question that comes to my mind is this: How do we know if we're suffering from this syndrome? The answer--We must allow Jesus to show us.

Jesus does this in the last part of Mark 12. We see Him standing in the Temple watching people bring their daily offerings. Many rich people place their offerings, and one poor woman places hers as well.

Jesus says, "This woman has no hypocrisy." She is not suffering from the hypocrite syndrome.

Here is a revealing truth: God has not called us to be spiritual headhunters. We see this in Matthew 13:24-30. We are to be people who focus on genuine love for God and for others. We must resist false living, and we must proclaim the gospel to all people.

One final question: Will heaven be filled with hypocrites or with poor widows? I believe the Scripture is clear. All who love Jesus will be there. We will be worshiping around the throne, and no, there will not be a section for hypocrites.

Here are our assignments for the week:

DAY 1:

Read Matthew 23 and answer the following questions.

1. How is it possible to teach God's Word but not live out God's Word?
2. How does a true Christian obtain greatness?

DAY 2:

Read Psalm 112 and answer the following questions.

- What are the characteristics of a blessed person?
- What does it mean to distribute freely?

DAY 3:

Read Psalm 110 and answer the following questions.

- Whom is David referring to in this chapter? Explain your answer.
- Has this prophecy already been fulfilled or is it still to come?

DAY 4:

Read 1 Timothy 3 and answer the following questions.

- How do these characteristics help us to better select church leaders?
- How are you challenged to pray for your pastors?

DAY 5:

Read Titus 1 and answer the following questions.

- Why do false leaders upset the church?
- How could someone profess to know God without wanting to serve Him? Explain.

End Times Imperatives

Scripture focus: Mark 13:1-13

*A*s *Jesus was leaving the temple, one of his disciples said to him, "Look, Teacher! What massive stones! What magnificent buildings!"*

"Do you see all these great buildings?" replied Jesus. "Not one stone here will be left on another; every one will be thrown down."

As Jesus was sitting on the Mount of Olives opposite the temple, Peter, James, John and Andrew asked him privately, "Tell us, when will these things happen? And what will be the sign that they are all about to be fulfilled?"

Jesus said to them: "Watch out that no one deceives you. Many will come in my name, claiming, 'I am he,' and will deceive many. When you hear of wars and rumors of wars, do not be alarmed. Such things must happen, but the end is still to come. Nation will rise against nation, and kingdom against kingdom. There will be earthquakes in various places, and famines. These are the beginning of birth pains.

"You must be on your guard. You will be handed over to the local councils and flogged in the synagogues. On account of me you will stand

before governors and kings as witnesses to them. And the gospel must first be preached to all nations. Whenever you are arrested and brought to trial, do not worry beforehand about what to say. Just say whatever is given you at the time, for it is not you speaking, but the Holy Spirit.

"Brother will betray brother to death, and a father his child. Children will rebel against their parents and have them put to death. Everyone will hate you because of me, but the one who stands firm to the end will be saved (NIV).

It seemed as if he would never land the plane. We were circling and circling apparently without even the thought of landing. Finally I leaned over to a friend and asked, "Will he ever land this plane?" About fifteen minutes later he landed it at last.

What was the problem? The pastor who was speaking didn't know how to wrap up his sermon. He kept trying to find a spot to land the sermon, but he could not.

Here in Mark 13 we see that this was not the case with Jesus. Jesus has landed the plane of debate and teaching in the Temple. He is leaving--right on time. Mark writes, "Jesus was leaving the temple."

Behind and beside Him were His trusted apprentices. As they came out of the Temple, Jesus was gearing up His mind for the Cross. But the apprentices were gearing up for what they believed would be a victory parade.

The apprentices take a moment to look at the glorious structure of the Temple. One of them comments, "What wonderful stones and buildings!" Could it be that they're thinking, "We will oversee this in the very near future"?

Jesus continues walking. The group crosses down through the Kidron Valley and then up to the Mount of Olives. Jesus sits down and begins to direct the apprentices' minds toward the future. The kingdom of God has come near, but the Kingdom's leader is about to go to the Cross. Israel's days of glory are not the focus of Jesus, but the day of victory for the world is in Jesus' sights.

As Jesus speaks to the apprentices, we see and hear His urgency as He speaks concerning the end times. The apprentices want to know how it will come to be, what will be the signs, and how they are to live in preparation for this time. Jesus gives us the answers in this text. This week you will have the joy of studying about the coming times and the signs of the times.

For just a moment I want to give you five imperatives given by Jesus that will lead you to be successful as the end draws near:

1. Do *not* be *led astray* by false leaders.

There were false leaders in Jesus' day and in our day as well. In Jesus' day were people who wanted Jesus' popularity and His position. Jesus says, "Do not follow such people."

2. Do *not* be *alarmed* by such days.

In our day it seems that many Christians are saying, "I'm worried about what will happen to us." Brothers and sisters, we do not have to worry--because Jesus is in charge.

3. Be *alert* to what's happening in your surroundings.

The apprentices would face hardship and imprisonment for their faith. This was God's sovereign choice for the furtherance of the gospel. These apprentices would stand before world leaders sowing and proclaiming the gospel.

4. Be *active* in these days.

As the world rages out of control there will be more and more windows for the gospel. Jesus challenges the church to be active in taking the gospel to the world. As we do, the gospel goes farther and farther until finally the last place on an earth with 7.7 billion people will have heard the gospel.

5. *Anticipate* the Lord's return.

Jesus could be returning even before this book is published. He could return before you finish reading this devotion. God is calling His people to a day of great anticipation because Jesus could return today.

Take these imperatives to heart as you spend this week focusing on end times.

Here are our assignments for the week:

DAY 1:
Read Jeremiah 14 and answer the following questions.
- What effect were the prophets having on their people?
- What effect are false prophets having in our day?

DAY 2:
Read John 8 and answer the following questions.
- What will happen to those who do not believe Jesus is the Son of God? Explain.
- What are Satan's favorite tactics in his attempt to destroy believers?

DAY 3:
Read Daniel 12 and answer the following questions.
- What was Daniel's "day of trouble?"
- What will be Daniel's "allotted place" in the end of days?

DAY 4:

Read Revelation 6 and answer the following questions.

- With the present turmoil in our nation, where does the United States fit in prophecy?
- Who is riding the white horse noted in Revelation 6?

DAY 5:

Read Luke 21 and answer the following questions.

- What does Jesus mean by referring to our opportunity to bear witness?
- Why are Christians affected by the unrest in our day, and what are their feelings about it? Discuss whether it is right or wrong to have such feelings.

WEEK FORTY-FOUR

What Time is it?

Scripture focus: Mark 13:14-37

"When you see 'the abomination that causes desolation' standing where it does not belong—let the reader understand—then let those who are in Judea flee to the mountains. Let no one on the housetop go down or enter the house to take anything out. Let no one in the field go back to get their cloak. How dreadful it will be in those days for pregnant women and nursing mothers! Pray that this will not take place in winter, because those will be days of distress unequaled from the beginning, when God created the world, until now—and never to be equaled again.

"If the Lord had not cut short those days, no one would survive. But for the sake of the elect, whom he has chosen, he has shortened them. At that time if anyone says to you, 'Look, here is the Messiah!' or, 'Look, there he is!' do not believe it. For false messiahs and false prophets will appear and perform signs and wonders to deceive, if possible, even the elect. So be on your guard; I have told you everything ahead of time.

"But in those days, following that distress,

"'the sun will be darkened,
and the moon will not give its light;

the stars will fall from the sky,
and the heavenly bodies will be shaken.'

"At that time people will see the Son of Man coming in clouds with great power and glory. And he will send his angels and gather his elect from the four winds, from the ends of the earth to the ends of the heavens.

"Now learn this lesson from the fig tree: As soon as its twigs get tender and its leaves come out, you know that summer is near. Even so, when you see these things happening, you know that it is near, right at the door. Truly I tell you, this generation will certainly not pass away until all these things have happened. Heaven and earth will pass away, but my words will never pass away.

"But about that day or hour no one knows, not even the angels in heaven, nor the Son, but only the Father. Be on guard! Be alert! You do not know when that time will come. It's like a man going away: He leaves his house and puts his servants in charge, each with their assigned task, and tells the one at the door to keep watch.

"Therefore keep watch because you do not know when the owner of the house will come back—whether in the evening, or at midnight, or when the rooster crows, or at dawn. If he comes suddenly, do not let him find you sleeping. What I say to you, I say to everyone: 'Watch!'" (NIV).

As the apprentices walked out of the Temple, the end of the journey was on their minds. Last week we focused on end time imperatives. The apprentices believed Jesus would rule and reign on the earth. Their view was correct. But their timing was off.

The apprentices looked at the Kingdom in terms of their lifetime. But Jesus looked at the Kingdom in terms of eternity. Almost two thousand years have passed since Jesus walked on the earth.

The question that occupies the church's mind today is the same as it was in that day: "When will Jesus come?"

Jesus makes four predictions in this week's Scripture focus. Each of them could occupy an entire week's worth of devotions. But we will focus on them in this one-time frame.

Jesus' first prediction takes in some of last week's Scripture focus: The gospel will be proclaimed in all the nations. As I write, there are over 11,000 people groups in our world. Still over half of these groups have never heard the gospel. But at the quickest rate in the history of the church, these groups are being penetrated with the gospel. First Baptist Church of Jackson is committed to globally being a part of fulfilling Jesus' prediction. Your Community Group is a part of this same work.

Jesus' second prediction speaks of the work of our enemy: The antichrist will attempt to rule the world. Under Satan's influence this world leader will attempt to unite the world under his political and religious power. He will be deceptive, and he will be deliberate in seeking to destroy the nation of Israel and its people. Jesus' warning to His chosen people is clear: "Get out of the nation now." When the time comes, you will know what Jesus said has come to be. You will see it.

Jesus' third prediction brings fear and sadness into the heart of everyone who believes the Bible: The Tribulation will be the most destructive seven years in the history of the world. Brothers and sisters, this is a bold statement when you consider all the destruction that has taken place in the history of the world. The world will be bent on self-destruction in the name of freedom and religion. The Lord says, "Unless I return all would be destroyed." Out of all the predictions, this is the one we see every day. As I am writing this devotion the headlines read of the destructive nature of humanity throughout our world. One online news agency had the following as their headline: "Syria still taking lives as the war rages on."

Jesus' fourth prediction is clearly to the point: He will return to rule and reign on the earth. As the Tribulation reaches its height of hatred, there is a sound of a mighty trumpet. The nations of the world have gathered for one last great battle. As they engage in the battle, suddenly the nations turn their attention heavenward as one riding a white horse is coming in the clouds. Who is this one? He is one they sing about as the Lion and the Lamb.

Could it be that Jesus is coming? Could we see this in our lifetime? The answer is simply that we won't know until we see Him. But what we see leads us to live in a way that is prepared to see Him.

We are to live a life that honors Him. We are to live a life with a ministry that is preparing to receive Him. We are to live on mission seeking to reach the world before He comes.

This week's readings will help to stir your heart for what you are seeing. In each day's readings you will hear the call "Stay awake."

Here are our assignments for the week:

DAY 1:
Read 2 Peter 3 and answer the following questions.
- Why has God waited so long to fulfill His promise in returning to the earth?
- What will happen to this world when Jesus returns?

DAY 2:
Read Revelation 16 and answer the following questions.
- What does it mean to "stay awake?" Explain.
- What is the city of Babylon in Revelation 16?

DAY 3:
Read Psalm 102 and answer the following questions.
- What types of prayers should we be offering in the days we live in?
- What or who is the one stabilizing force in our changing world?

DAY 4:

Read Joel 2 and answer the following questions.

- What will the day of the Lord look like from your understanding of Joel 2?
- Why was Joel calling the people to return to the Lord?

DAY 5:

Read Luke 21:34-38 and answer the following questions.

- What are the devil's weapons to keep us busy in these last days?
- What is the church doing to help people to be prepared for the day?

Beauty in a War Zone

Scripture focus: Mark 14:3-9

*W*hile he was in Bethany, reclining at the table in the home of Simon the Leper, a woman came with an alabaster jar of very expensive perfume, made of pure nard. She broke the jar and poured the perfume on his head.

Some of those present were saying indignantly to one another, "Why this waste of perfume? It could have been sold for more than a year's wages and the money given to the poor." And they rebuked her harshly.

"Leave her alone," said Jesus. "Why are you bothering her? She has done a beautiful thing to me. The poor you will always have with you, and you can help them any time you want. But you will not always have me. She did what she could. She poured perfume on my body beforehand to prepare for my burial. Truly I tell you, wherever the gospel is preached throughout the world, what she has done will also be told, in memory of her" (NIV).

Sometimes the most beautiful things occur in the most unlikely places. For example, in the middle of a world war couples meet and are brought together in a moment of agony. Such begins a marriage that lasts a lifetime.

Before us this week is a war zone (the days leading up to Jesus' death). The apprentices have been invited to the home of a man simply known as Simon the Leper. Jesus is the guest of honor. Also, the guest list includes Mary, Martha, and Lazarus.

Most believe Mark simply named the host because the first-century believers were very familiar with his story. Some scholars believe he was the leper who came to Jesus in Mark 1:40-45. One thing is for sure. He is no longer a leper. So we see a miracle house with mercy (Jesus) being the guest of honor. Ministry is occurring as they are honoring Jesus.

Keep in mind that outside the walls of Simon's house is a war zone. Just up the road a few miles is Jerusalem, getting ready for Passover. The city is deeply divided about Jesus. Soon Jesus will go to the Cross. But in this moment, beauty arises from an unlikely place.

One of the women (Mary) arises from her place at the table and does the unlikely. Look at her hands. She is holding a small stone flask with a long, slender neck. The flask has never been opened. It holds about one pint of expensive ointment found from a small rare plant native to India. The worth of that one pint is valued at one year's worth of wages.

Suddenly the aroma in the room changes. We see Mary breaking open the top of the small-neck stone flask. The smell quickly fills the room. Mary gently pours the ointment onto Jesus' head as a sign of honor. Next, according to John's account, she pours some onto His hands and feet. Last, she wipes Jesus' feet with her hair.

Brothers and sisters, this is beauty in a war zone.

What do we gain here? No fewer than four points:

1. This is a loving act of giving back to Jesus the best she owned.

2. This is a beautiful act of worship.

3. This is a picture of what is to come. Mary anoints Jesus' body before the Cross.

4. This is an example for each of us.

Have we given our best to Jesus? Before we answer that, we need to see the other side, the dark side of the war zone.

Mark tells us of the anger that is stirred up in the apprentices' hearts. They are indignant over what has happened. The NRSV says they "said to one another in anger" (verse 4). In our next devotion we will see what is behind this dark side. But for now it is clear that the apprentices are caught up in the hyprocosy of sin.

How often do you and I get caught up in dark responses to beautiful moments? How about when someone cries out in worshipful praise to God? Do we get angry because he or she is disturbing our quiet worship? How about when someone does things a little differently? How about when we meet people who are a little different than we are? Do we simply label them as strange and then walk away?

God extends mercy to all people. Those who embrace Jesus' mercy experience the new birth. This new birth leads them into a new way of life.

God blessed Mary because she worshiped with her best. That's what God wants from you and me. Our best is what God blesses for His glory. In this broken world our God is looking for people who will love as Mary loved. Are you one of those people?

Here are our assignments for the week:

DAY 1: READ
Psalm 23 and answer the following questions.
- What acts of mercy has the Great Shepherd worked in your life?
- Who does it mean when the Psalmist writes, "Thou hast anointed my head with oil"?

DAY 2:

Read John 12 and answer the following questions.

- What was Judas's real problem?
- What problems do you and I have with unique moments of worship?

DAY 3:

Read 1 Corinthians 14 and answer the following questions.

- What gifts has God given you for His glory? List them please.
- Why do we sometimes fail to seek spiritual gifts? Explain your answer.

DAY 4:

Read Philippians 2 and answer the following questions.

- What did Jesus sacrifice in coming to the earth?
- What did Paul mean by "being poured out like a drink offering" (verse 17, NIV)?

DAY 5:

Read Leviticus 18 and answer the following questions.

- Why were the people instructed to worship as they were in Leviticus 18?
- What do other people think when they see you worshiping the Lord?

"Judas" – the Name Says it All

Scripture focus: Mark 14:10-11

Then Judas Iscariot, one of the Twelve, went to the chief priests to betray Jesus to them. They were delighted to hear this and promised to give him money. So he watched for an opportunity to hand him over (NIV).

With Holy Spirit precision, Mark leads us down the path of Jesus' last days leading up to the Cross. This week's Scripture focus lands us on a moment that is given only two verses in all of Mark's writings, but these two verses speak to us about a moment that has been well known by many in every generation.

Here we are given information about the coming-out party of a present apprentice. The man's name says it all, simply "Judas." He is one of the original twelve apprentices. He has been allotted a share of the apprentice work, that of treasurer of the group.

Very quickly we discover Judas's heart. This apprentice is all about the money. I believe Judas was attracted to the group but was not all-in with the group. He was for the earthly kingdom being established, but he was not going to get into the cross-bearing thing. It is noteworthy that Judas would have been in the group for at least one year before Jesus began speaking about the Cross. From the start, Judas was taking advantage of his position as treasurer (John 12:6). He was always embezzling funds from the group.

By this moment in Mark 14, Judas knew that his attachment to Jesus was about to get complicated. If he stayed in the group things could turn out badly for him. I believe he saw one last opportunity to make a buck from his position as an apprentice.

Just before Judas launches his plan, a scene occurs in John 12, noted in last week's devotion, in which Mary shows her love for Jesus by breaking open an expensive bottle of perfume to anoint Jesus with. Was it in this moment that Judas says, "This is enough"? What could have triggered such a response from Judas?

I believe this was truly a deep hurt for the other apprentices as they tried to make sense of what Judas did. In Acts 1 we see how God leads them to move beyond Judas' betrayal. But what happened to Judas?

Did this man lose his faith? Did he ever have genuine faith? Did Jesus lose a good man to the dark side?

Brothers and sisters, we do not have to speculate or try to read between the lines of Scripture to gain our answer. The answer is in Luke's account. Here it is: "Satan entered into Judas" (Luke 22:3). Little by little and day by day, Judas gave himself over more and more to Satan. Finally came the day when Judas did not even consider saying no to Satan.

This week you will read stories about people who gave in to the enemy's attacks. I pray that this week's studies will help you to understand the danger of playing around with the enemy.

Here are some Judas facts:

1. Judas was never a true believer. He was a lost man who associated with Jesus but was not all in with Jesus.

2. Judas was living a lie. He seemed to have accepted Jesus, but he was only around Jesus.

3. Judas loved his lies. He enjoyed taking advantage of his position, but it did him no eternal good.

4. Judas was lost for all eternity. He gave away Jesus to the priests, and he gave his soul to Satan.

Question: What will the facts say about our names?

Here are our assignments for the week:

DAY 1:

Read 2 Samuel 14 and 15 and answer the following questions.

- What led to Absalom's betrayal of his father?
- What could David have done differently?

DAY 2:

Read Judges 11 and answer the following questions.

- What type of leader was Jephthah? Explain.
- Why did Jephthah make such a rash vow?

DAY 3:

Read Genesis 25 and answer the following questions.

- What type of character did Esau possess?
- What was Esau's disposition toward his family?

DAY 4:

Read Numbers 12 and answer the following questions.

- Why did Moses' siblings rebel against his leadership?
- Why did God judge Miriam so severely?

DAY 5:

Read Numbers 16 and answer the following questions.
- What happened in Korah's rebellion?
- Why did God stand with Moses?

We Will Remember

Scripture focus: Mark 14:12-25

On the first day of the Festival of Unleavened Bread, when it was customary to sacrifice the Passover lamb, Jesus' disciples asked him, "Where do you want us to go and make preparations for you to eat the Passover?"

So he sent two of his disciples, telling them, "Go into the city, and a man carrying a jar of water will meet you. Follow him. Say to the owner of the house he enters, 'The Teacher asks: Where is my guest room, where I may eat the Passover with my disciples?' He will show you a large room upstairs, furnished and ready. Make preparations for us there."

The disciples left, went into the city and found things just as Jesus had told them. So they prepared the Passover.

When evening came, Jesus arrived with the Twelve. While they were reclining at the table eating, he said, "Truly I tell you, one of you will betray me—one who is eating with me."

They were saddened, and one by one they said to him, "Surely you don't mean me?"

"It is one of the Twelve," he replied, "one who dips bread into the bowl with me. The Son of Man will go just as it is written about him. But woe to that man who betrays the Son of Man! It would be better for him if he had not been born."

While they were eating, Jesus took bread, and when he had given thanks, he broke it and gave it to his disciples, saying, "Take it; this is my body."

Then he took a cup, and when he had given thanks, he gave it to them, and they all drank from it.

"This is my blood of the covenant, which is poured out for many," he said to them. "Truly I tell you, I will not drink again from the fruit of the vine until that day when I drink it new in the kingdom of God" (NIV).

In the front section of my childhood church stands a table before the pulpit. That table has stood there for decades and is well worn with use. But the writing on the front side of the table remains clear: "In remembrance of me."

As a kid I looked at the table so many times without considering the truth of what was written. As an apprentice of Jesus, I admit that I sometimes still fail to remember what the Lord's Supper means.

This week's Scripture focus takes us back to the moment when Jesus institutes this important event. Mark begins his retelling by setting the date in time: "It was the first day of Unleavened Bread." This means on this day, Passover will come at evening time.

This will be Jesus' third Passover with the apprentices. It will be His last. It will be at this Passover Feast that Jesus completes what the Passover had been anticipating. Each year God's people would sacrifice a lamb for the sins of the family as a symbol of their looking forward to the day when the Lamb of God would come.

As the apprentices sit around the table with Jesus, the Lamb of God is about to be slain. The apprentices are about to hear words from Jesus that will shake them.

While reclining at the table Jesus says, "One of you will deny me this night." You and I know the scene has already been set, because Judas has already set it up. Eleven of the disciples are in shock. Each wonders, Is it I? Judas knows it is him, but to save face (Matthew 26:25) he asks, "Is it I?" Jesus responds: "You have said so."

Quickly Mark moves into the moment we want to remember, one the church looks back to, one that the church has claimed as the basis of one of its precious ordinances.

As I read these words, I think back over forty-three years of participating in what the apprentices first experienced on the night of His betrayal. Never has the Lord's Supper been so real to me. Watch as Jesus lifts the bread, breaks it, and gives a piece to each apprentice. This is a picture of Jesus' body that will be broken for the sins of humanity. Jesus takes our sin so that we can take His righteousness (2 Corinthians 5:21). Jesus knows He will face the wrath of God in our place (Revelation 1:7).

As the apprentices eat the bread, do they understand it all? Do you and I remember as we take the bread that Jesus went through the worst treatment a body could endure? Do you and I know the weight that Jesus felt, having never known sin?

Before the apprentices can respond, Jesus lifts the cup and then passes it to each apprentice. This is a picture of Jesus' blood, which would be spilled out on the heavenly altar for our sins (1 John 1:7). By His blood you and I can be cleansed from our sin.

I see the apprentices considering the glorious eyes of the Son of God. I see them as they try to process all this. Suddenly Jesus says, "Do this in remembrance of me."

I can honestly say as I write this devotion that I want to take the Lord's Supper. I want to experience the sweet fellowship of God and the sweet unity with God's people as I take the Lord's Supper.

This week I want to challenge you to focus on three wonderful truths as you work through the assignments:

1. Jesus was going to the Cross for you and me.

Allow yourself to study deeply all that the Lord's Supper means for you. Keep in mind what Jesus promised: "Someday I will eat this supper with you."

2. Jesus would conquer the Cross for you and me.

Jesus would come out of the grave, would ascend to the Father, and someday will come again. Oh, what a day that will be!

3. Jesus will meet us through the Holy Spirit at the Lord's table this coming Sunday.

Here are our assignments for the week:

DAY 1:

Read Luke 22 and answer the following questions.

*   Why was it so difficult for the apprentices to figure out that Judas was the betrayer?
*   What happens when a person takes the Lord's Supper?

DAY 2:

Read Joshua 5 and answer the following questions.

*   Why had Israel failed to keep the Passover supper during the forty years of wilderness wandering?
*   Why do we sometimes forget the Lord's Supper in our churches today?

DAY 3:

Read 1 Corinthians 11 and answer the following questions.
- Why was the church in danger of being judged by God?
- What is your church's viewpoint about the Lord's Supper?

DAY 4:

Read Revelation 22 and answer the following questions.
- Will there be a need for the Lord's Supper in heaven?
- How could a properly conducted Lord's Supper challenge people to come to Jesus?

DAY 5:

Read Psalm 143 and answer the following questions.
- How does the Lord's Supper give us assurance of God's forgiveness of our sins?
- How many reasons can you find in the Lord's Supper for praising the Lord? List some below.

More than You Can Handle

Scripture focus: Mark 14:26-42

*W*hen *they had sung a hymn, they went out to the Mount of Olives.*

"You will all fall away," Jesus told them, "for it is written:

> *"'I will strike the shepherd,*
> *and the sheep will be scattered.'*

But after I have risen, I will go ahead of you into Galilee."

Peter declared, "Even if all fall away, I will not."

"Truly I tell you," Jesus answered, "today—yes, tonight—before the rooster crows twice you yourself will disown me three times."

But Peter insisted emphatically, "Even if I have to die with you, I will never disown you." And all the others said the same.

They went to a place called Gethsemane, and Jesus said to his disciples, "Sit here while I pray." He took Peter, James and John along with him, and he began to be deeply distressed and troubled. "My soul is overwhelmed with sorrow to the point of death," he said to them. "Stay here and keep watch."

Going a little farther, he fell to the ground and prayed that if possible the hour might pass from him. "Abba, Father," he said, "everything is possible for you. Take this cup from me. Yet not what I will, but what you will."

Then he returned to his disciples and found them sleeping. "Simon," he said to Peter, "are you asleep? Couldn't you keep watch for one hour? Watch and pray so that you will not fall into temptation. The spirit is willing, but the flesh is weak."

Once more he went away and prayed the same thing. When he came back, he again found them sleeping, because their eyes were heavy. They did not know what to say to him.

Returning the third time, he said to them, "Are you still sleeping and resting? Enough! The hour has come. Look, the Son of Man is delivered into the hands of sinners. Rise! Let us go! Here comes my betrayer!" (NIV).

As we open our Bibles to this week's Scripture focus, the last thing on our minds would be the Cross. It is the Christmas season. However, we must be reminded that the reason He came was to die in our place.

The apprentices have now been with Jesus for three-plus years. The moment is both deflating and draining to their lives. The hour is, by most conservative estimations, after midnight. Their mental and physical tanks are likely on "E."

The hymn they sing would encourage them. I can see them with high hopes of victory as they cross over the Kidron Valley one more time. Once again, the apprentices find themselves in a familiar place. In this moment we feel maybe the hunger of the men to go on to sleep.

Jesus speaks: "Tonight each of you will desert me."

The apprentices' responses are typical of anyone who is in disbelief. These guys have walked with Jesus through good times and bad times. They would not even consider such a possibility. Yes, they have been weak in faith and sometimes have completely blown it with Jesus. But they are still with Him. Denying Jesus is the farthest thing from their minds. But what seemed impossible does indeed happen on this night.

Here is a point that we must grasp: There are moments in life when we come up against things that are more than we can handle. In these moments we must trust them to God's hands.

Peter speaks: "The others may desert you, but not me."

Jesus speaks: "Peter, you will deny me."

In this moment Peter could have cried out, "Lord, have mercy!" or "Lord, help me!" But he does not. In this moment the little rock was about to fall off the big rock.

Mark, as he does so well, moves directly to the next scene. Here we see Jesus in the garden with His apprentices. They have been here before, but never with this intensity. Jesus settles down seven disciples and asks them to pray. He then takes Peter, Andrew, James, and John deeper into the garden. He asks them to watch and pray with Him.

In this moment the men are giving way to pressure that is more than they can handle. You and I are familiar with such pressure. Jesus begins offering agonizing prayer as He prepares to have the sin of the world placed upon Him. Within the next twelve hours Jesus will endure the complete wrath of God. He asks, "Is there any other way?" In this passionate scene, Jesus accepts the will of God the Father.

He returns to the apprentices to find them sleeping. This happens three times. The first time Jesus awakens Peter with a question: "Could you not hold out one hour in prayer?" This is not a put-down but a statement of truth. Peter is beyond his limits. He needs to be alert to the devil's path, and he needs to cry out for God's mercy and power.

It is true--the apprentices have nothing left to give, but it is the opposite with God. He is limitless in His power to save. When this group needed Jesus the most, they found themselves choosing to look to the flesh and abandon the Spirit.

There's a strong lesson for you and me in this story. We must become a people who confess our powerlessness, and we must claim His power.

This week our assignments will place us in Scripture that will amplify this truth. May God bring you to the end of yourself this week so that when you are weak--He will be strong!

Here are our assignments for the week:

DAY 1:
Read Isaiah 40 and answer the following questions.
- What causes believers to become spiritually weak?
- What does Isaiah mean by being able to "mount up with wings like eagles"?

DAY 2:
Read Zechariah 13 and answer the following questions.
- What would cause the sheep to scatter?
- Who are the people who are being refined?

DAY 3:
Read 2 Corinthians 12 and answer the following questions.
- What was Paul's "thorn in the flesh"?
- What power does God offer each believer?

DAY 4:
Read Psalm 29 and answer the following questions.
- Why does God's voice have so much power? Explain.
- What do you need God's voice to speak to in your life? Write your answers.

DAY 5:

Read Matthew 26 once again and answer the following questions.

- Describe how Peter must have felt when he heard the rooster crow the second time.

- How hard is it for the believer to be restored?

After Dark

Scripture focus: Mark 14:43-72

*J*ust *as he was speaking, Judas, one of the Twelve, appeared. With him was a crowd armed with swords and clubs, sent from the chief priests, the teachers of the law, and the elders.*

Now the betrayer had arranged a signal with them: "The one I kiss is the man; arrest him and lead him away under guard." Going at once to Jesus, Judas said, "Rabbi!" and kissed him. The men seized Jesus and arrested him. Then one of those standing near drew his sword and struck the servant of the high priest, cutting off his ear.

"Am I leading a rebellion," said Jesus, "that you have come out with swords and clubs to capture me? Every day I was with you, teaching in the temple courts, and you did not arrest me. But the Scriptures must be fulfilled." Then everyone deserted him and fled.

A young man, wearing nothing but a linen garment, was following Jesus. When they seized him, he fled naked, leaving his garment behind.

They took Jesus to the high priest, and all the chief priests, the elders and the teachers of the law came together. Peter followed him at a distance, right into the courtyard of the high priest. There he sat with the guards and warmed himself at the fire.

The chief priests and the whole Sanhedrin were looking for evidence against Jesus so that they could put him to death, but they did not find any. Many testified falsely against him, but their statements did not agree.

Then some stood up and gave this false testimony against him: "We heard him say, 'I will destroy this temple made with human hands and in three days will build another, not made with hands.'" Yet even then their testimony did not agree.

Then the high priest stood up before them and asked Jesus, "Are you not going to answer? What is this testimony that these men are bringing against you?" But Jesus remained silent and gave no answer.

Again the high priest asked him, "Are you the Messiah, the Son of the Blessed One?"

"I am," said Jesus. "And you will see the Son of Man sitting at the right hand of the Mighty One and coming on the clouds of heaven."

The high priest tore his clothes. "Why do we need any more witnesses?" he asked. "You have heard the blasphemy. What do you think?"

They all condemned him as worthy of death. Then some began to spit at him; they blindfolded him, struck him with their fists, and said, "Prophesy!" And the guards took him and beat him.

While Peter was below in the courtyard, one of the servant girls of the high priest came by. When she saw Peter warming himself, she looked closely at him.

"You also were with that Nazarene, Jesus," she said.

But he denied it. "I don't know or understand what you're talking about," he said, and went out into the entryway.

When the servant girl saw him there, she said again to those standing around, "This fellow is one of them." Again he denied it.

After a little while, those standing near said to Peter, "Surely you are one of them, for you are a Galilean."

He began to call down curses, and he swore to them, "I don't know this man you're talking about."

Immediately the rooster crowed the second time. Then Peter remembered the word Jesus had spoken to him: "Before the rooster crows twice you will disown me three times." And he broke down and wept (NIV).

Yes, it is true, things look radically different after dark. Consider the following. When I was a kid I would spend all day outside in the yard, but as soon as darkness came I would not go outside alone.

Have you ever considered why things are so radically different in the night? Jesus taught about this in John 3:16-21. But now they are seeing it firsthand on this night where they are already facing more than they can handle.

Maybe you're finding yourself in an after-dark moment. It could be the darkness of facing the holidays without a loved one or knowing that a broken relationship leaves you without the hope of getting together at Christmas. Maybe you're short on funds this holiday season, or maybe you're facing a different type of crisis.

Mark presents four scenes in the after-dark moments of the apprentices.

- The darkness of betrayal and arrest (verses 43-50)

Jesus sees the coming mob. He knows it is time for the Cross. Judas is the betrayer, but Jesus is in charge. This is a moment of grace, because Jesus knowingly comes to this moment. It is a moment of miracle, when Jesus restores the ear of one in the mob. Suddenly the night is not so dark because we see the sovereign control of the Lord.

- The darkness of getting caught (verses 51-52)

We see Mark as a courageous young man who in the moment is caught but is able to get away. Suddenly the night takes on new meaning, as we realize how easy it is for us to run when emotion takes over.

- The darkness of a crooked trial (verses 53-65)

The moment of darkness is a set up for Jesus. The tribunal has already made up their minds and has the sentence ready before the trial begins. Jesus is humbly facing this dark moment.

Jesus is calm, committed, and clear in this moment of trial. He affirms the truth--"I am the Son of God. I will die. I will be buried. I will rise again, and I will ascend back to the throne of my Father." Suddenly the night takes on new meaning again. Jesus' darkness was the segue to victory. It can be the same for us!

- The darkness of denial (verses 66-72)

So many times I have been through this passage, and so many times I have lived out its after-dark experience with others. How many teenagers have faced this same courtyard experience after dark?

This moment is more than Peter can handle. If only he would have humbled himself before the Lord (1 Peter 5:6-7). Peter is amid hand-to-hand combat with the forces of hell. He wants to go all the way with Jesus, but his emotions are pulling him apart. He is afraid, and he will be ashamed.

Please do not be condemning of our brother, one of the twelve apostles. Peter faced the greatest of after-dark moments. He failed, but he would be restored. He was broken, but afterward he would become a leader who would in another dark moment become the greatest of examples of faithfulness.

It is still yet to be determined as to what you and I will do after dark. One thing is clear: if we walk in the light as He is the light, we will not fail! James Froude wrote these powerful words: "The worth of a man must be measured by his life, not by his failure under a single and peculiar trial."

Here are our assignments for the week:

DAY 1:

Read John 18 and answer the following questions.
- Why did the mob draw back and fall when Jesus spoke?
- Why did Peter act so courageously before the mob and then so cowardly before the people at the campfire?

DAY 2:

Read Acts 13 and answer the following questions.
- Why did Mark leave Paul and Barnabas?
- What would cause a believer to become silent in his or her faith? Give some examples.

DAY 3:

Read John 1 and answer the following questions.
- According to John the Baptist, who is Jesus?
- Who was Jesus in eternity past?

DAY 4:

Read Proverbs 15 and answer the following questions.
- According to verse 13, what happens when our spirits are crushed?
- According to verse 32, did Peter ignore God's instructions for this moment in the darkness?

DAY 5:

Read John 21 and answer the following questions.
- Why did Peter decide to go fishing?
- How hard was it for Peter to see Jesus the first time after his denial?

WEEK FIFTY

Not What You Expected

Scripture focus: Mark 15

*V**ery early in the morning, the chief priests, with the elders, the teachers of the law and the whole Sanhedrin, made their plans. So they bound Jesus, led him away and handed him over to Pilate.*

"Are you the king of the Jews?" asked Pilate.

"You have said so," Jesus replied.

The chief priests accused him of many things. So again Pilate asked him, "Aren't you going to answer? See how many things they are accusing you of."

But Jesus still made no reply, and Pilate was amazed.

Now it was the custom at the festival to release a prisoner whom the people requested. A man called Barabbas was in prison with the insurrectionists who had committed murder in the uprising. The crowd came up and asked Pilate to do for them what he usually did.

"Do you want me to release to you the king of the Jews?" asked Pilate, knowing it was out of self-interest that the chief priests had handed Jesus over to him. But the chief priests stirred up the crowd to have Pilate release Barabbas instead.

"What shall I do, then, with the one you call the king of the Jews?" Pilate asked them.

"Crucify him!" they shouted.

"Why? What crime has he committed?" asked Pilate.

But they shouted all the louder, *"Crucify him!"*

Wanting to satisfy the crowd, Pilate released Barabbas to them. He had Jesus flogged, and handed him over to be crucified.

The soldiers led Jesus away into the palace (that is, the Praetorium) and called together the whole company of soldiers. They put a purple robe on him, then twisted together a crown of thorns and set it on him. And they began to call out to him, *"Hail, king of the Jews!"* Again and again they struck him on the head with a staff and spit on him. Falling on their knees, they paid homage to him. And when they had mocked him, they took off the purple robe and put his own clothes on him. Then they led him out to crucify him.

A certain man from Cyrene, Simon, the father of Alexander and Rufus, was passing by on his way in from the country, and they forced him to carry the cross. They brought Jesus to the place called Golgotha (which means "the place of the skull"). Then they offered him wine mixed with myrrh, but he did not take it. And they crucified him. Dividing up his clothes, they cast lots to see what each would get.

It was nine in the morning when they crucified him. The written notice of the charge against him read: THE KING OF THE JEWS.

They crucified two rebels with him, one on his right and one on his left. Those who passed by hurled insults at him, shaking their heads and saying, *"So! You who are going to destroy the temple and build it in three days, come down from the cross and save yourself!"* In the same way the chief priests and the teachers of the law mocked him among themselves. *"He saved others,"* they said, *"but he can't save himself! Let this Messiah, this*

*king of Israel, come down now from the cross, that we may see and believe."
Those crucified with him also heaped insults on him.*

At noon, darkness came over the whole land until three in the afternoon. And at three in the afternoon Jesus cried out in a loud voice, "Eloi, Eloi, lema sabachthani?" (which means "My God, my God, why have you forsaken me?").

When some of those standing near heard this, they said, "Listen, he's calling Elijah."

Someone ran, filled a sponge with wine vinegar, put it on a staff, and offered it to Jesus to drink. "Now leave him alone. Let's see if Elijah comes to take him down," he said.

With a loud cry, Jesus breathed his last.

The curtain of the temple was torn in two from top to bottom. And when the centurion, who stood there in front of Jesus, saw how he died, he said, "Surely this man was the Son of God!"

Some women were watching from a distance. Among them were Mary Magdalene, Mary the mother of James the younger and of Joseph, and Salome. In Galilee these women had followed him and cared for his needs. Many other women who had come up with him to Jerusalem were also there.

It was Preparation Day (that is, the day before the Sabbath). So as evening approached, Joseph of Arimathea, a prominent member of the Council, who was himself waiting for the kingdom of God, went boldly to Pilate and asked for Jesus' body. Pilate was surprised to hear that he was already dead. Summoning the centurion, he asked him if Jesus had already died. When he learned from the centurion that it was so, he gave the body to Joseph. So Joseph bought some linen cloth, took down the body, wrapped it in the linen, and placed it in a tomb cut out of rock. Then he rolled a stone against the entrance of the tomb. Mary Magdalene and Mary the mother of Joseph saw where he was laid (NIV).

"This was supposed to be a week where I got so much accomplished, but it has not turned out as I expected it to." This was the discouraged commentary given by a mother who ended up spending part of the week in the hospital with a sick child. As she sat there in the hospital, she pulled up her to-do list on her iPad. The list was full. She was supposed to go shopping on Monday and complete the purchase of last-minute gifts. She was going to pick out a Christmas tree on Tuesday and decorate the house on Wednesday. Thursday was marked for cookie day. In this moment the mother felt the weight of her week. Under her breath she said, "This was not what I expected!"

Question: How is your week going?

I'm always amazed by the fact that the enemy does his best to destroy every holiday and every plan we have in life. The apprentices of Jesus find themselves experiencing what they did not expect on Passover weekend.

Our focal text reveals to us no fewer than six crushing moments in Jesus' day. Christian historians label this day as "Good Friday." To the naked eye this seems like a ridiculous label. But a deeper look reveals this truth: "And I, when I am lifted up from the earth, will draw all people to myself" (John 12:32).

The day begins with Jesus facing the condemnation of the Jewish council (Mark 15:1-5). Pilate is brought into the mix and attempts to deliver Jesus, but the wishes of the corrupt council win the day (verses 6-14). Jesus is given into the hands of the cruel Roman legion (verses 15-20). He is beaten and physically mistreated beyond my ability to describe. Look at Jesus. Was this a day He did not expect? How can we compare our tough week to His tough week?

If all this were not enough, now Jesus is led to be crucified and is placed on the cross at 9 AM. For the next six hours Jesus is on the cross.

Mark writes about the crowds that file by the cross, saying, "If you are God, come down from the cross." The religious leaders promise to believe in Jesus if He would miraculously come down.

Think through this with me. How often have we prayed, "Lord, if you will remove this tough moment, I will serve you"? How many times have we said, "Lord, I will do whatever you want if you will remedy this . . ."? But nothing happens. Is this because God is not able, or is it that He knows better what we really need?

On this day the world did not need Jesus to come off the cross. The world needed for Jesus to stay on the cross! At noon darkness comes over Golgotha's hill. This is a darkness unlike any that has ever been seen. God is covering His eyes from Jesus, who is taking on himself the sins of the world, facing the wrath of God.

During the Christmas season most people forget about the darkness of the world. They're kinder and willing to help others. But still the truth remains--the world is a dark place where people are dying without Jesus. Only the blood of Christ can remove the darkness of sin.

In these three hours Jesus purchases our redemption. At the end of these three hours He cries out and breathes His last. John 19:30 records His last words: "It is finished." Yes, it is true things did not turn out as the apprentices thought, but they did turn out as God said they would.

We see Jesus being taking down from the cross, and Joseph of Arimathea takes his stand for Jesus. He steps up and asks for the body. As evening comes, the sun begins setting and the night starts coming forth. Jesus is placed in the garden tomb and the stone is laid before the door.

As we stand there with the women looking at the garden tomb, it hurts because things have not turned out as we thought. Listen carefully: "Weeping may endure for a night, but joy cometh in the morning" (Psalm 30:5, KJV).

I want to challenge each of you to look beyond the pain of the moment and focus on the purpose of the moment. God will accomplish what you do not expect with what you do not expect!

Here are our assignments for the week:

DAY 1:
Read Psalm 6 and answer the following questions.
- How can you identify with what the Psalmist is enduring in the psalm? Explain.
- Why did the Psalmist bring his hurt before the Lord?

DAY 2:
Read Psalm 68 and answer the following questions.
- How does God bear up His people (verse 19)? Explain.
- How much power does God have? Why do we sometimes seem to be powerless?

DAY 3:
Read Ezra 8 and answer the following questions.
- What danger did Ezra and his people face as they sought to obey the Lord?
- Why was Ezra ashamed to ask the king for a band of soldiers and horseman to protect them?

DAY 4:
Read 2 Chronicles 15 and answer the following questions.
- Why will the Lord not be with His people?
- What does it mean to seek the Lord?

DAY 5:
Read Matthew 1 and Luke 1. Answer the following questions.
- How would you have felt if you had been Joseph when things did not work out as you expected?
- Why does God sometimes not do things as we expect and in the ways we expect? Explain.

WEEK FIFTY-ONE

Easter in December

Scripture focus: Mark 16:1-10

When the Sabbath was over, Mary Magdalene, Mary the mother of James, and Salome bought spices so that they might go to anoint Jesus' body. Very early on the first day of the week, just after sunrise, they were on their way to the tomb and they asked each other, "Who will roll the stone away from the entrance of the tomb?"

But when they looked up, they saw that the stone, which was very large, had been rolled away. As they entered the tomb, they saw a young man dressed in a white robe sitting on the right side, and they were alarmed.

"Don't be alarmed," he said. "You are looking for Jesus the Nazarene, who was crucified. He has risen! He is not here. See the place where they laid him. But go, tell his disciples and Peter, 'He is going ahead of you into Galilee. There you will see him, just as he told you.'"

Trembling and bewildered, the women went out and fled from the tomb. They said nothing to anyone, because they were afraid.

When Jesus rose early on the first day of the week, he appeared first to Mary Magdalene, out of whom he had driven seven demons. She went and

told those who had been with him and who were mourning and weeping
(NIV).

As I pick up my pen to write this chapter, I realize Christmas is here. I also realize the Scripture focus before us is about Easter. The question that comes to my mind is this: How do I write about Easter in December?

I actually don't know of many people who talk about Easter in in this last month of the year. Now I remember one of my ministers of music who used to have "Christmas in July" as he began his practices with the choir for a Christmas musical. But how do we talk about Easter in December? Answer: We do it with the reality that Jesus' coming is all about the cause of Easter.

As Jesus' apprentices, we know the great value of Jesus' first coming. Without it, of course, Easter would not have been possible. One athlete put his running career in perspective when he said, "Unless I crossed each starting line, I had no hope of crossing each finish line." So today we say, "Thank you, Jesus for coming." But we also need to say, "Thank you for staying and purchasing for us the gift of redemption."

For a few moments let's travel back in time to that first Easter Sunday morning.

I imagine the three women coming together, and no doubt they had planned this when they had left the garden tomb (Mark. 15:47) just before the Passover. They possibly met at the eastern gate of the city to make their way out to Jesus' tomb as the sun was peaking up over the Jerusalem hillside. They hugged each other tightly as they gave and received comfort from each other. The disciples were in hiding, but these women, moved with love in their hearts, made their way to the tomb. I hear Salome saying, "I still can't believe this happened." Mary the mother of Jesus responds, "I finally understand what the old gentlemen meant years ago when he said that a sword would pierce my heart through" (Luke 2:33-35). The other Mary begins to silently weep for what seemed like the hundredth time. They walk along silently. Now they're coming up to the cemetery and the question comes: "Who will roll the stone away for us?" Will the guards help, or will they even let them see the body of Jesus? The feeling among the women is sorrow beyond what human words can describe.

Now they are at the tomb. But things are not as they thought they would be. The guards are passed out, and the stone has been rolled away. Should they run away or should they look inside? Our answer comes from the angel who is there: "Do not be afraid. You seek Jesus of Nazareth. He is not here. As He said, He has risen. Come and see the place where He lay."

Brothers and sisters, everything changed for these three women. A few moments ago they were in heartbreak, but now their hearts beat again with the joy of knowing Jesus is alive. This is the truth we must remind ourselves in these sometimes-depressing days of Christmas.

You will meet people who are standing on the stone of unbelief this Christmas season. They do not believe in the Christmas story. Pray that God uses you to show them the truth of the gospel so that the stone will be rolled away.

You will meet people who are standing on the stone of fear this Christmas season. Reach out to them and show them the love of Christ so that they will understand we serve a God who is worth coming out for.

You will also meet people who are slipping from the stone of faith this Christmas season. Their dreams have been dashed through some dark moment. This Christmas can be their moment of light if you lead them to the God of Easter.

I want to challenge you to read all the passages closely this week. Correlate them in your studies. Write down your observations, and be ready to make application for all you meet. Help people around you as Jesus' apprentices.

Your devotions and assignments for the week are as follows:

DAY 1:

Read Matthew 28 and answer the following questions.

- If you had been one of the guards at the tomb, how would you have felt about what you saw? Explain.
- How important is Jesus' birth to the story of Easter? Explain your answer.

DAY 2:

Read Luke 24 and answer the following questions.

- How do you explain "the living among the dead"?
- Why was it so hard for the two people traveling on the road to Emmaus to recognize Jesus? Explain your answer.

DAY 3:

Read John 20 and answer the following questions.

- How does Thomas's first response to the news of Jesus' death mirror the response of much of the world? Explain your answer.
- How can Mary's encounter with Jesus give encouragement to people who struggle with depression during the Christmas season?

DAY 4:

Read 1 Corinthians 15 and answer the following questions.

- According to this chapter what is the greatest gift Jesus gave to the world? Explain.
- Did Jesus have the Cross in mind when He was coming to the earth? Explain.

DAY 5:

Read 1 Thessalonians 4 and answer the following questions.
- What are you looking forward to in the coming year? Explain.
- What from this past year are you thankful for? Explain.

WEEK FIFTY-TWO

The End of the Beginning

Scripture focus: Mark 16:11-20

*W*hen they heard that Jesus was alive and that she had seen him, they did not believe it.

Afterward Jesus appeared in a different form to two of them while they were walking in the country. These returned and reported it to the rest; but they did not believe them either.

Later Jesus appeared to the Eleven as they were eating; he rebuked them for their lack of faith and their stubborn refusal to believe those who had seen him after he had risen.

He said to them, "Go into all the world and preach the gospel to all creation. Whoever believes and is baptized will be saved, but whoever does not believe will be condemned. And these signs will accompany those who believe: In my name they will drive out demons; they will speak in new tongues; they will pick up snakes with their hands; and when they drink deadly poison, it will not hurt them at all; they will place their hands on sick people, and they will get well."

After the Lord Jesus had spoken to them, he was taken up into heaven and he sat at the right hand of God. Then the disciples went out and preached everywhere, and the Lord worked with them and confirmed his word by the signs that accompanied it (NIV).

Yyou made it! Yes, you did! You have come to the last week of our journey as fellow apprentices at the feet of Jesus. The last fifty-two weeks have been filled with so much life change. Now it's time to set our sights on what I have called "the end of the beginning."

Think back to our first week at the feet of Jesus. In that week we wanted to know, "Who could this be, the one they called Jesus?" I asked you on this first week together to write down what you knew about Jesus. Now, fifty-two weeks later, I ask you to do it again.

Let's discover how our views have changed.

Last week we considered Jesus' last recorded words with the apprentices.

The setting is immediately following the Resurrection. Jesus will spend forty days with the disciples and then return to heaven (Acts 1:8). We know little detail of what type of instruction takes place those forty days, but what we do know is extremely significant. Jesus gives the apprentices, and all who will be apprentices, the assignment of gospel proclamation to the entire world. Again, this is the end of the beginning.

As we encounter the apprentices we find them at a difficult place. Literally they are facing the agony of a broken heart. Twice we read of these men hearing the good news of Jesus' resurrection, and twice they refuse to believe.

It is important for every apprentice to have a clear and committed heart to accomplish the assignment of God. I wonder if the apprentices felt like the Psalmist in Psalm 69:20--"Reproaches have broken my heart, so that I am in despair. I looked for pity, but there was none, and for comforters, but I found none."

When your heart is broken it is truly impossible to move into a new day. Maybe as you come to the end of this year you find your heart broken by the events of this year. Allow me to challenge you this week to do what the apprentices did:

- They had an encounter with Jesus that gave them closure with the past.

- They heard from Jesus in a way that gave them purpose for the present.

- They received power from Jesus so they could accomplish their purpose.

This encounter had been ongoing for three-plus years. Now it would be even more intense as the Holy Spirit would reside within them, teaching them all that Jesus had taught them (John 16).

I want to challenge you to commit yourself to a daily encounter with Jesus in the new year. I want to challenge you to listen each day to His daily assignment for your life. I want to challenge you to walk in the power of the Spirit as you face each new day.

Your devotions and assignments for the week are as follows:

DAY 1:

Read Deuteronomy 7 and answer the following questions.
- Why did God choose Israel?
- What Did God want Israel to do?

DAY 2:

Read Romans 9 and answer the following questions.
- What happened to Israel?
- Where do the Gentiles fit in to God's plan?

DAY 3:

Read Acts 1 and write down the places where you have already shared the gospel.

DAY 4:

Read Ephesians 6 and offer prayer for your church to be able to fulfill the Great Commission.

DAY 5:

Read Acts 13 and answer the following questions.

- Was it hard to let go of two of the best leaders in the church? Explain.
- What areas of your life is God burdening you about?
- What will you and God do next year?